Who's in Charge Here?

JOHN HUFFMAN, JR.

Who's in Charge Here?

Foundations of Faith From Romans 1-8

CHRISTIAN HERALD BOOKS
Chappaqua, New York

We acknowledge with appreciation permission to quote from:
Fiddler on the Roof, copyright 1964, The Times Square Music Publications Company. All rights reserved. Used by permission.

Library of Congress Cataloging in Publication Data

Huffman, John A.
  Who's in charge here?

  1. Bible. N.T. Romans I-VIII—Criticism, interpretation, etc. I. Title.
BS2665.2.H83   227'.107   81-65721
ISBN 0-915684-84-5   AACR2

MEMBER OF
EVANGELICAL CHRISTIAN
PUBLISHERS ASSOCIATION

Christian Herald, independent, evangelical, and interdenominational, is dedicated to publishing wholesome, inspirational, and religious books for Christian families.

First Edition
CHRISTIAN HERALD BOOKS, 40 Overlook Drive,
Chappaqua, New York 10514
Printed in the United States of America

DEDICATION

This book is written with deep appreciation to:

The St. Andrew's congregation,
which so lovingly went through
the stretching process with me

Many biblical scholars
upon whose writings
I have depended for guidance

My good friend Bill Chickering,
who encouraged me to publish my work
and helped me so much in the editing

Contents

Ashamed of the Gospel? 1

For I am not ashamed of the gospel: It is the power of God for salvation to everyone who has faith, to the Jew first and also to the Greek. For in it the righteousness of God is revealed through faith for faith; as it is written, 'He who through faith is righteous shall live' (Romans 1:16-17).

FOR FIFTEEN YEARS I've been telling myself that some day I'll be prepared to write something about the book of Romans. That day of preparedness has never arrived. I realize now that I'll never *feel* ready, never *feel* adequate. That's because Romans speaks too forcefully to me on some of the more stark and base facts of my nature that I would just as soon avoid. No one enjoys being confronted with his sin.

No one has ever faced the truths in the book of Romans and remained the same. No church has been exposed to the full light of its teachings without making a decision as to whether or not it will content itself with popular, romantic, sentimental Christianity or whether it will move on to the often harsh, yet purifying realities of what it truly means to be a gathering of the people of God, justified by faith and growing through the sanctifying influence of the Holy Spirit.

Romans is "reality therapy." In it we see ourselves in the mirror of God's truth. The image is not a pleasant one. It is not pleasant because something in us will bear witness to its correctness. It is only through this awareness, however, that God will be able to remake us, conforming us to His image.

Many years ago, Dr. Donald Grey Barnhouse began his

9

ministry at the Tenth Presbyterian Church in Philadelphia. He had decided that he should preach through the book of Romans. I don't know how long he planned to take on the series, but it took him over three years to finish. The first Sunday he preached for one hour on Romans 1:1. The second Sunday he preached one hour on Romans 1:2 but didn't say all that he felt needed to be said about that verse. He ended up devoting the third week to finishing up the second verse of the first chapter.

The story of what God did in the life of Dr. Barnhouse, and in the lives of those in his congregation, is history. The main floor of the sanctuary began to fill with people who were hungry for spiritual reality. Soon the balcony also filled. Week after week the crowds came in great numbers to hear the uncompromising message of Romans.

Anyone who wishes to begin a thorough study of a book of the Bible must first find the answers to four basic questions: 1. Who wrote the book? 2. To whom was the book written? 3. When was the book written? 4. Why was the book written? We may not always have a precise answer to some of these questions, but we must explore them if we wish to have a full understanding of the book we have chosen to study.

Who wrote the book of Romans?

It was written by Paul, who identifies himself as a man whose life has been set apart to perform three specific functions.

First, he calls himself a "servant of Jesus Christ." A more realistic translation of that word is "slave." He acknowledged Jesus Christ to be his master, his owner. Paul knew something that non-Christians, as well as a lot of professing Christians, have not grasped—that not until we can honestly call ourselves slaves of Jesus will we ever experience the knowledge of the freedom which that slavery offers.

He calls himself an "apostle." Not only does he recognize Jesus Christ as his master, he is aware that he has been given a charge by the God of the universe. He is an ambassador. He is a representative of God empowered to carry God's message.

Finally, he calls himself one who is "set apart for the gospel." He sees that he is different. He knows that the calling he has received is not handed out lightly. The message he has been set apart to convey is so important that he must be willing to sacrifice and suffer for it.

And sacrifice and suffer he did. The Gospel proved very costly to Paul: Five times he had been beaten thirty-nine lashes. Three times he had been beaten with rods. Once he was stoned. Three times he had been shipwrecked. He'd been exposed to raging rivers, robbers, sleepless nights, hunger, thirst, cold, and exposure. Paul was not embarrassed or ashamed, no matter how foolish or forlorn he may have appeared to others. He was convinced that the radical life change of those who heard the Gospel would be worth the price.

To whom was the book of Romans written?

Romans was written as a letter to a group of Christians living in Rome, the most powerful city in the known world at that time. Paul was writing to Christians living in a city governed by dissipated emperors who had godlike powers conferred upon them and who used their power to serve the causes of public and private corruption. It was a city that had a slave population of over 600,000.

The believers in Rome were people Paul had never met. He had only heard about them. The things he heard must have been favorable, for he wrote, "I thank my God through Jesus Christ for all of you, because your faith is proclaimed in all the world (Romans 1:8).

When did Paul write this letter to the Roman Christians?

The letter was written about twenty-three years after

the resurrection and ascension of Jesus. Paul was in Corinth, near the end of his third missionary journey. He was staying at the home of Gaius and would soon be carrying a relief offering to the church at Jerusalem.

If Rome was the most powerful city in the world, Corinth was the most decadent. You can visit the museum in Corinth and see artifacts which underline the immorality of that ancient port city.

Paul would walk the streets of Corinth, brushing past four or five thousand people, many of whom were temple prostitutes who mixed sexual immorality with their religious worship. He observed the materialism, the crude acquisitiveness which viewed human value on the basis of how much a person owned. He watched as people cheated one another in the market place. Husbands double-timed their wives. Masters took advantage of their slaves. In fact, some scholars have written that Paul probably wrote his letter to Rome from a second- or third-story room overlooking the market place, dictating to his secretary, Tertius, while watching the kinds of activities you could have seen, and can still see, on Sunset Boulevard in Hollywood or in Times Square in New York City. Paul was a student of human behavior, an astute one. That's how he could write so candidly about the depth of depravity to which human beings will go when they cut themselves off from the God who loves them.

Why did Paul write to the Roman Christians?

First, to let them know how much he desires to see them. Romans 1:8-15 tells of how often he had intended to visit them, but through either one circumstance or another has been waylaid.

I doubt if Paul ever won an award for diplomacy or tact. He was blunt. He didn't play politics with his utterances. However, there was something that marked his attitude which those of us who call ourselves Christians need to cultivate. Paul had a tremendous sense of love and a need to be in communion and fellowship with other Christians. He yearned to involve himself in the lives of others. He wasn't afraid to express his affection for other believers.

I'm very much aware of the dangers of psychological manipulation. I've seen public speakers who have exploited audiences with compliments, making them feel so good about themselves that they will do what the speaker wants them to do. Then, behind the scenes, they laugh at the gullibility of their audiences.

Paul's expressions of affection are not manipulative. He is aware that no one touches another person's life with the Gospel of Jesus Christ unless the speaker's heart engages the heart of the listener, unless the writer's heart engages the heart of the reader. That is part of the reason why we, as a secularist, non-Catholic country, so embraced John Paul II. We sensed his love. His teachings were tough teachings, teachings that even many members of his church did not accept. But he spoke them honestly, with the heart of a pastor, a friend, a representative of God.

But the audience must also be sensitive. Paul had detected on the part of the church at Rome a loving and caring spirit. He longed to be with them because of the vitality of their faith. No audience ever listens with any profit from a preacher if that audience comes in with preconceived notions, carping criticism, cold indifference, or aloofness. There needs to be mutual affection.

Second, Paul wrote this letter in order to review and clarify the terms of salvation. He wanted to see the believers strengthened in their faith. Paul saw himself as the transmitter of the message of grace. He didn't say to the Roman Christians, "I'm going to strengthen you." He wanted to give them a gift that they might be strengthened.

Paul knew that the Christians at Rome would face ideological bombardment from groups that proposed to have found an answer other than Jesus Christ. He writes so that they will stand firm and not be swayed.

Third, Paul writes because he has a dream, and he wants his readers in Rome to be a part of that dream. Paul was a missionary at heart. He had a vision — to be a planter of churches wherever he traveled. He knew that the church at Rome was in good shape and that he was not needed to conduct a "church growth" seminar.

Paul wanted to go and preach in Spain. His work at Greece was completed. He tells the believers at Rome, "This is the reason why I have so often been hindered from coming to you. But now, since I no longer have any room for work in these regions, and since I have longed for many years to come to you, I hope to see you in passing as I go to Spain, and to be sped on my journey there by you, once I have enjoyed your company for a little" (Romans 15:22-24).

Paul's ministry was subject to discouragement and conflict. He knew that he needed the believers in Rome — he needed their encouragement. Although the Scriptures do not say it clearly, I'm sure that he also needed their financial support.

After his introduction, Paul moves on through the next eight chapters with a discussion of the great doctrines of the Christian faith. But just before beginning that discussion Paul does precisely what the presiding officer at a national convention does. He picks up a gavel and bangs it on the lectern. He states boldly, "For I am not ashamed of the gospel: it is the power of God for salvation to every one who has faith, to the Jew first and also to the Greek. For in it the righteousness of God is revealed through faith for faith; as it is written, 'He who through faith is righteous shall live.'" Paul, who had been imprisoned at Philippi, chased out of Thessalonica, smuggled out of Berea, laughed at in Athens, who in Corinth said that his message is foolishness to Greeks and a stumbling block to Jews, shouts a loud declaration, "I am not ashamed!"

These final verses of the introduction briefly mention the themes that will wind their way through his letter.

First, the Gospel. The Gospel is the good news promised by God through His prophets in the Old Testament. The Gospel is the incarnation, God become man to live among us, the atonement, the suffering and death of Jesus on the cross as payment for our sin, and the resurrection, Jesus' physical rising from the dead, His triumph over death and sin.

Second, the power of God. The study of Romans will be an exercise in futility if we do not see ourselves as empowered by God through the Gospel. The Holy Spirit is able to energize us, to give us the strength and the insight and the wisdom, to give us all we need to live creatively and harmoniously with God, ourselves, and our neighbor.

Third, is salvation. Is there anything that the world yearns for more than salvation? What if you knew that you could be saved from an eternity without the love of God to comfort you, saved from the wrath of God and his judgment (judgment that we deserve!)? Doesn't that elevate the often trite expression, "Are you saved, brother?" to something more meaningful than a buttonholing evangelistic technique?

Fourth, is faith. Paul says that it is offered to all people, the Jew as well as the Gentile. It makes no difference. We do not have to earn it. The fact is, we can't earn it. You and I can never score enough points through our good works to earn God's favor. God sees us only through the blood of His Son, whom we accept by faith. Paul tells us that it is through faith that the righteousness of God is revealed, and it is through faith that we become righteous. We can never justify ourselves or make ourselves righteous, though we often try. Our efforts at playing God in these areas are pitiful and futile.

Righteousness is God's to give, not ours to attain. God tells us that our attempts at "self"-righteousness are as "filthy rags" — things to be thrown out with the rubbish. Yet we continue striving, spurning God's offer of grace.

Paul concludes his introduction by saying, "He who through faith is righteous shall live." Another way of saying that is, "The just shall live by faith."

Though Paul wrote the letter to the Romans to clarify some important matters of doctrine, it should not be viewed in that light alone. Its intention is also to show us the nature of God — who He is and what He has done for us. Paul wants us to be able to say with him, "I am not ashamed."

Creature Worship **2**

Therefore God gave them up in the lusts of their hearts to impurity, to the dishonoring of their bodies among themselves, because they exchanged the truth about God for a lie and worshiped and served the creature rather than the Creator, who is blessed forever! Amen (Romans 1:24-25).

SOME OF US don't like bluntness, yet we want to know how things really are. We'd turn to another channel every night if Walter Cronkite came on giving birth notices, wedding congratulations, and listing fiftieth wedding anniversaries. Good news is a valid part of life. But so is bad news.

Romans 1:18-32 is a blistering analysis of the depraved nature of mankind. It's a fact of life we need to see. It's only against the stark backdrop of reality that we confront the glory of what God has done for us in Jesus Christ.

Have you ever shopped for a diamond? Have you noticed what the jeweler does before he displays one of those precious stones? He lays a black cloth on top of the counter. He places the gems on that stark, contrasting background. That way you get a good look at what the stone is really like. You're free to concentrate on it. The darkness eclipses other sensory stimulations which could compete for your attention.

Paul writes, "For the wrath of God is revealed from heaven against all ungodliness and wickedness of men who by their wickedness suppress the truth" (Romans 1:18). God hates all ungodliness, all wickedness. His wrath is not just some cosmic outburst. It is a sustained, settled, condition. God stands in holy contrast to all attitudes and actions that run counter to His will.

17

Dietrich Bonhoeffer, that perceptive German theologian, who faced death because he had the courage to counter Hitler, refers to "a next to the last word" which must be heard and experienced before you can hear the "last word" of God's grace in Jesus Christ. Law precedes grace. He wrote about this in *Letters and Papers from Prison*:

> It is only when one submits to the law that one can speak of grace, and only when one sees the anger and wrath of God hanging like grim realities over the head of one's enemies that one can know something of what it means to love them and forgive them. I don't think it is Christian to want to get to the New Testament too soon and too directly. We have often talked about this before, and I am more than ever convinced that I am right. You cannot and must not speak the last word before you have spoken the next to last.

Let's look at the progression that mirrors why mankind is in its present mess.

God has revealed Himself in nature. Paul writes, "For what can be known about God is plain to them, because God has shown it to them. Ever since the creation of the world his invisible nature, namely, his eternal power and deity, has been clearly perceived in things that have been made. So they are without excuse; for although they knew God they did not honor him as God or give thanks to him, but they became futile in their thinking and their senseless minds were darkened" (Romans 1: 19-21).

Everyone has a chance to look at the evidence. There's something deep inside of every human being which says that there is more to life than chance. There must be a God who brought it all into being.

Psalm 19: 1-4 states it clearly, "The heavens are telling the glory of God; and the firmament proclaims his handiwork. Day to day pours forth speech, and night to night declares knowledge. There is no speech, nor are there words; their voice is not heard; yet their voice goes out through all the earth, and their words to the end of the world." All nature cries out that this is no accident. Our consciences tell us that there is right and that there is wrong. What has mankind done? Paul says in Romans 1:18 that men "by their wickedness suppress the truth." He goes on to say, "For although they knew God they did not honor him as God or give thanks to him" (Romans 1:21).

Paul is saying that stamped on all of nature is the fact that there is a God who created. Mankind has chosen to go his own way, and is therefore without excuse. In fact, Paul tells us that mankind has made a very clear choice. The choice is revealed in Romans 1:25. He says, "They exchanged the truth about God for a lie and worshiped and served the creature rather than the Creator, who is blessed forever! Amen."

Creature worship. Our miserable human predicament is brought about by the fact that we worship the creature rather than the Creator. We have bought a lie. Some of us have kidded ourselves into thinking that there is no God — while God lives on. And much more subtly, there is a constant pressure in the human race to create new gods which are, in reality, "no gods" because they are creatures. Paul shows us that there are three tragic results that emerge when we exchange the truth about God for a lie.

First, creature worship is idolatry. When we dethrone the Creator God, there is that religious nature within us all that has to have some kind of god to worship. Our first tendency is to latch on to ourselves. Paul says that when mankind switches from confidence in divine wisdom to human wisdom, there is a futility in thought and that senseless minds are darkened.

Nowhere do we see a clearer indication of this than in the area of politics. In our lifetime, we've seen manmade

schemes that promised a beautiful era. We've had the New
Deal, the Fair Deal, the New Society, the New Frontier,
Peace with Honor, detente, and God only knows what the
next big promise will be. But we always buy it. It's fascinating to see the way we functioned as a nation. We
knocked a president out of office because he was dishonest. We elected a president because we basically felt he
was a sincere, honest man. Now we've knocked that
president out of office because we felt he wasn't compe-
tent enough. The latest opinion polls say that the average
American would now prefer to have a dishonest president
than an honest president if that dishonest man was compe-
tent. We're gullible enough that we're just liable to end up
with a president who is both dishonest and incompetent.
God says that's what happens when we put our confidence
in man. "Claiming to be wise, they became fools" (Romans 1:22).

And then we see a descending spiral of idolatry. Not
only do we put human beings on a pedestal, worshiping
our own minds and what we can accomplish, we forget
that whatever we can accomplish results from the fact that
we are created in the image of God. Our worship is subject
to a devolution in which we go from worshiping man to
worshiping images that look like man. From that we move
on to birds, and then to animals, and finally to reptiles.
The worship of reptiles is the lowest form of creature
worship. At that point we have given our homage to that
which ultimately produces a fear reaction.

What is it that you worship? What in your life do you
idolize most? Is your idol your family? Is it your career? Is
it your political viewpoint?

Has your religion become an idol? There is that tendency to wear a label, whether it be Presbyterian, Methodist,
or Baptist; whether it be evangelical, liberal, or orthodox.
We can allow these labels to become the objects of our

worship, instead of the living God who created us to worship Him.

Second, sexual immorality is a direct result of creature worship. Paul writes, "For this reason God gave them up to dishonorable passions. Their women exchanged natural relations for unnatural, and the men likewise gave up natural relations with women and were consumed with passion for one another, men committing shameless acts with men and receiving in their own persons the due penalty for their error" (Romans 1: 26-27).

This is a sensitive area. Several denominations have recently gone through a terrible struggle on the topic of homosexuality. Interestingly enough, it isn't mentioned that often in the Scriptures. When it is, homosexual practice is called sin, an abomination, a sign of the depths to which Creator worship has become distorted by creature worship.

But it's easy to lift out one orientation to sin that is alien to many of us and nail persons of this orientation to the wall, when the Bible is just as specific about other sexual orientations such as the desire for sexual intercourse with a member of the opposite sex, be it premarital or extramarital. You see, the orientation or temptation toward a certain action is not sin. However, to practice fornication, adultery, or homosexuality is sin. And interestingly enough, to be so threatened by persons who do these things so as to hate them is also sin. Our sexuality is one of our most precious gifts from the Lord and is one of the first things to go off kilter when we are living in creature worship. The conscience tells us that there is something wrong with sexual expression outside of the man/woman relationship in which there is commitment to exclusive faithfulness through marriage. The Scriptures reinforce this and make it explicit, telling us that it's the only smart way to live.

Third, Paul moved on to be just as explicit about other kinds of wickedness produced by creature worship.

Six years ago, I was invited to address a "Moral Decency Rally" in Miami, Florida. Ten thousand people were gathered in the Miami Beach Convention Center. I had flown down from Pittsburgh for the event, joining several national radio and television personalities. This rally took place during the Dade County referendum on the homosexual issue that pushed the name of Anita Bryant into the headlines. I shared a concern with other people that militant gays should not be allowed to redefine for society what is right conduct and what is wrong conduct, while the church sits silent. However, I was appalled as I listened to several noted clergy step to the pulpit, open the Bible to Romans 1, and begin to castigate persons of homosexual orientation. With hostility and anger, they elevated both the practice and the orientation to a position of being the most heinous and despicable sins of all. Frankly, those men hadn't done their homework. They had lifted a couple of verses out of the Scripture, forgetting the context.

There are other activities in which we find ourselves practicing creature worship. Paul writes, "And since they did not see fit to acknowledge God, God gave them up to a base mind and improper conduct. They were filled with all manner of wickedness, evil, covetousness, malice. Full of envy, murder, strife, deceit, malignity, they were gossips, slanderers, haters of God, insolent, haughty, boastful, inventors of evil, disobedient to parents, foolish, faithless, heartless, ruthless. Though they know God's decrees that those who do such things deserve to die, they not only do them but approve those who practice them" (Romans 1: 28-32).

When we devolve into creature worship we find ourselves caught up in the grocery list of practices enumerated for us by Paul. Not for a moment is he noting one sin as the most wicked of all. He places alongside homosexual practice and murder some other sins, which may not seem as bad to our finite minds, but which express an identical disobedience to God. He talks about gossip, boastfulness, and disobedience to parents.

The point is clear. Creature worship in its most blatant or most subtle practice is death-producing. It's at the base of all sin. It's our pride that says, "I'll worship who and what I want to worship. I'll be who and what I want to be. I can do a pretty good job of doing as I please."

Do you see yourself? I sure see myself! There's that Watergate, that Chappaquiddick in us all. We all have our deceptions. The sad thing is that we've bought into them and try to persuade others to believe in them.

Earl Palmer, pastor of the First Presbyterian Church in Berkeley, California, has written a commentary on the book of Romans titled *Salvation by Surprise*. He says that the tragedy of the human race consists in the breakdown and distortion of the vital relationships of man. Relationship one is to God. We are caught up in a hostility toward Him that produces idolatry.

Relationship two is to self. We're confused as to who we are and that produces the sexual inversion and immorality that runs so rampant. So we live in a state of hell, isolated, alone, in what C.S. Lewis calls an "infinite distance from every other person."

Relationship three is to the rest of the created order. Whether we like it or not, this is a moral universe. If we worship the creature rather than the Creator, the Creator gives us up to the sad results. That's what it means to be exposed to the wrath of God. This passage tells us that God gave them up in the lust of their hearts to impurity. It tells us that God gave them up to dishonorable passions. It says that God gave them up to a base mind and to improper conduct. The second to last is that God gave us up to hell, both in this life and in the life to come.

But there is a last word. The last word is not bad news, it's good.

Both the bad news and the good news are capsuled in these words that Paul wrote to the church at Corinth: "Do you not know that the unrighteous will not inherit the kingdom of God? Do not be deceived; neither the immoral, nor the idolaters, nor adulterers, nor sexual perverts, nor thieves, nor the greedy, nor drunkards, nor revilers, nor robbers will inherit the kingdom of God. And such were some of you. But you were washed, you were sanctified, you were justified in the name of the Lord Jesus Christ and in the Spirit of God" (1 Corinthians 6: 9-11).

That's why Paul is not ashamed of the Gospel. He knows that it is the power of God for salvation to all who have faith. Grace comes only when we see ourselves as hell-bound sinners, who can't break the cycle in our own power, who are twisted and bent toward creature worship — with all of the idolatry, and immorality, and gross wickedness which that produces — but who have repented and put our trust in Jesus Christ, who, through His death and resurrection, has paid the price of our sin and now is willing to clothe us in His righteousness.

That's the good news. That's the final word.

Judgmentalism and Judgment 3

Therefore you have no excuse, O man, whoever you are, when you judge another; for in passing judgment upon him you condemn yourself, because you, the judge, are doing the very same things (Romans 2:1).

WHENEVER we see the horrible result of man's rebellion against God, there are those of us who recoil. We compare ourselves with others and conclude that we're not that bad. Out of this comes the cancer of judgmentalism.

Can you see the picture? Standing aloof from the whole mess is a very religious person. He stands there looking down into a pit filled with sinners of the most disgusting nature. His posture connotes superiority. He condescendingly prays, "I thank my God that I am not like those awful people. Look at them. They worship birds and snakes. I don't worship idols. I have no homosexual drives. I've never committed adultery. I've never stolen. And I attend First Reformed, Bible Believing, Orthodox, Evangelical Holiness Church right here in my home town. Paul turns right around and says, "Hey, you're involved in this mess, too. Whoever you are, you who judge are in much more subtle ways doing the same things."

In Romans 2: 1-16, Paul focuses on two critical themes. First, he talks about judgmentalism. Then, he speaks about the judgment of God.

I

Judgmentalism is the most deadly and cancerous sin of all.

25

What sin did Jesus single out more than any other? Was it theft? Was it adultery? Was it murder? No. It was self-righteousness. It was that tendency within each of us to make judgmental comparisons with others.

It's my biggest sin. I want to look good. I want to impress people that I've done my best. And the only way people are going to be impressed is for me to make myself look better than others — usually at their expense. The result is a pride, a conceit, a self-righteousness.

It's almost impossible to be a preacher without appearing to be self-righteous. Most of us who genuinely want to do what is right succumb to this tendency. We also easily assume the provincialism of the Pharisee who looked down on the sin of others while failing to recognize his own.

Some of you who are from the Southeast will relate to this whimsical commentary by John MacLean, a Southern Presbyterian pastor and native of eastern North Carolina. You'll appreciate this if you've ever spent any time in Virginia or the Carolinas. It's the prayer of the modern Pharisee.

> I thank thee, Lord, that I am a North Carolinian and not from Virginia or South Carolina, those two mountains of conceit bordering the vale of humiliation, full of pompous pride and unaware that their progressive neighbors have long ago out-distanced them; and I thank thee, Lord that I am an eastern North Carolinian, for is it not a proverb that, "No gentleman was ever born west of tidewater?" Especially, Lord, I thank thee that I am a Southerner and not a Yankee — for there are many things one might endure, but not that! Grateful am I, O Lord, that I am a North American, and not a South American, for there is a vast difference, as everybody knows; and that I was born in these favored United States and not in Mexico or Canada. I thank thee, Lord, that I am a Gentile and not a Jew. Yes, of course, Jesus was born a Jew and many others of

that race were princes in Israel when my ancestors were Nordic barbarians, but that has been a long time ago. Why bring that up now? I thank thee that I am white, not yellow or red or brown or black. The Bible does teach that "While man looketh on the outward appearance, God looketh on the heart," but the outward appearance counts for a lot below the Mason-Dixon line.

I thank thee, O Lord, that I am a Protestant and not a Roman Catholic. Yes, it is a fact that for hundreds of years — long before anyone had ever thought of a Protestant Church — the Catholics kept alive the light of the Christian faith, and my denomination no longer brands the Pope as that "antichrist...and son of perdition." But anyway, put it to my credit that I am a Protestant. And, Lord, I thank thee that I am a Presbyterian, and not — well, one hesitates to be too specific — but after all, we Presbyterians are educated, or used to be, and we do feel that it is nice to be "just right," not "high-hat" like the Episcopalians, not yet so, shall we say, provincial or narrow as the Baptists or Methodists? Yes, naturally, there are some Presbyterians who are not what they ought to be, but they are mostly in the Northern branch. I thank thee, Lord, that I am a Southern Presbyterian, yes, and eastern-North Carolinian, North American, occidental, Scots, Gentile, white, civilized, Protestant, Southern Presbyterian! What a man!

Don't we all in our own ways have some of these feelings of superiority, if for no other reason to perhaps cover our own sense of inadequacy?

I made a mistake early in my marriage. Being from Boston and marrying a southern Californian, I got a big kick out of telling my in-laws, "There's not a good library west of the Mississippi. And if I ever really got sick, the only place I'd ever want to be treated would be in Boston by a Harvard Medical School graduate." I don't think they have ever forgotten that condescending statement.

Jesus had a way of fingering our weaknesses. He did it through the use of hyperbole. He would state a spiritual truth and then drive it home with an exaggerated illustration. For example:

> Judge that you not be judged. For with the judgment you pronounce you will be judged, and the measure you give will be the measure you get. Why do you see the speck that is in your brother's eye, but do not notice the log that is in your own eye? Or how can you say to your brother, "Let me take the speck out of your eye," when there is the log in your own eye? You hypocrite, first take the log out of your own eye, and then you will see clearly to take the speck out of your brother's eye (Matthew 7:1-5).

This would be a humorous picture, if it weren't so true. Jesus is saying that those of us who are most religious, or consider ourselves to be most religious, have the tendency to nit-pick. We get real close to someone else and look for that microscopic speck in their eye, while we have a rafter or a beam sticking out of our own head. Every time we move around, we knock someone over with it. He's suggesting that in the area of judgment we pay a little more attention to ourselves than to our neighbor.

Our Lord does call for us to have a spirit of discernment. He follows this immediately by saying, "Don't give dogs what is holy; and do not throw your pearls before swine" (Matthew 7:6). We are not to be gullible persons, oblivious to the sins of others to the point that we find our own lives drawn into improper attitudes and practices. To discern what is wrong in others without seeing ourselves as intricately involved in the same types of alienation, creates serious trouble.

Judgmentalism is the one sin you'll find everywhere. You'll find it in the lowest and highest of circles — the boardroom and the barroom. You'll meet it in the prayer group or in the locker room. It has a way of sneaking into the all-night prayer meeting as well as the slumber party. It's our way of cutting others down to size so we can look bigger and better.

Ultimate creature worship is self-righteousness. That's why Paul Tournier, a Swiss psychiatrist, emphasizes that Christianity is the only religion in the world which says that God loves the unrighteous more than the righteous.

Think about that. *The biggest problem Jesus had was with self-righteous people*. The self-righteous person dooms himself, for he finds his salvation in himself. He worships his own accomplishments and attitudes.

Another way of putting this is that there is overt and covert sin. The woman caught in adultery was thrown at the feet of Jesus. Her captors had discovered her in the act of sin. It's fascinating to see that she was actually more open to forgiveness than her holier-than-thou accusers whose sins were more covert. Their sins were under wrap. But the gaze of Jesus bore through that cover. He called their bluff. He challenged them, urging the one among their numbers who was without sin to cast the first stone. The Mosaic Law said death by stoning was the penalty for adultery. When the light shifted from overt to covert, these men couldn't stand the glare and they slunk away.

What's the bottom line on judgmentalism? Paul puts it in these words: "We know that the judgment of God rightly falls upon those who do such things. Do you suppose, O man, that when you judge those who do such things and yet do them yourself, you will escape the judgment of God? Or do you presume upon the riches of his kindness and forbearance and patience? Do you not know that God's kindness is meant to lead you to repentance?" (Romans 2: 2-4).

God calls you and me to repentance. He calls us to be sorrowful for our sin. He calls us to a desire to turn around and proceed in a new direction. He calls us to put aside that comparative approach to Christianity by which we derive our sense of well-being at the expense of our neighbor. He calls us to come to God in genuine worship, with a contrite spirit, acknowledging the hopelessness of our situation apart from Him.

II

Fact one. The very fact that we judge each other shows that we do have a conscience. The deceitfulness of the human heart is strikingly exhibited by our double standard — pulling others down as we attempt to exalt ourselves. What we're doing is "plea bargaining." We know that there are inadequacies in our lives. But by making our sin appear small compared to the sin of another, we somehow feel we have been vindicated.

The tendency of a religious person is to see God as good-naturedly indifferent to sin. This is not what the Scriptures teach. Ours is a God whose heart is broken by sin, yet He is also a God who, by the nature of His holiness, must not look askance at our wrongdoing. Romans 2:16 underlines the fact of the judgment, letting us know that some day we will stand responsible before God: "On that day when, according to my gospel, God judges the secrets of men by Christ Jesus."

The Word of God says that we "have no excuse" (Romans 2:1). The Word of God tells us that when we judge others, and yet have rebelled against God ourselves, there is "no escape." We are told that the secrets of our lives will be revealed when we stand before Jesus Christ. To pretend that this will not happen is pure sentimentality. Deep in our hearts we all know that there is a law of accountability. You can only kite checks so long, until the bank finally calls and informs you that your account has got some serious problems.

Fact two. Each of us will be judged according to our

deeds. "For he will render to every man according to his works" (Romans 2:6). God is not a respecter of persons. Whether you are a Jew or Gentile will make no difference. You are responsible to stand before Him. "For God shows no partiality" (Romans 2:11). Righteousness does not come through religiosity. You will stand without it on the judgment day and you will be looked at according to your deeds.

Fact three. The judgment of God will be also in accordance to the light each person has enjoyed. Paul writes, "All who have sinned without the law will also perish without the law, and all who have sinned under the law will be judged by the law" (Romans 2:12). This proves the justice of God. The ground of the judgment is our works. The rule of the judgment is the light which we have been given. Those of us who have been exposed to God's special revelation through the Scriptures will be judged by that standard. We'll have no excuse. God's Word has been very specific with us.

Is the main theme coming across? Sin is the cause of death. We can try to make ourselves look good by making others look bad. We can, in the process, destroy ourselves by this judgmentalism. We're kidding no one but ourselves. God is impartial. He is straightforward. He will judge us according to His holiness.

When He looks at you and asks you what right you have to enter the kingdom of heaven, what are you going to say? Is your answer, "I tried to live a good life and did a lot better than this list of people here with whom I constantly compared myself"? Will you say, "I served as an elder. I taught in the Sunday school. I sang in the choir. What do you think I am, some kind of pagan? I was a very religious person"? According to the Scripture, Jesus would have to shake His head and say on the basis of what you've thus far said, you have no right to enter His kingdom. He could make a cosmic display of all the secrets, all the cover-ups, all the attitudes you've held, all the covertness of your existence.

It could be a very embarrassing moment, couldn't it? You've no excuse. There's no escape from what you've done, until you suddenly remember, you remember that the Christian faith was not derived for those who were already righteous. Christianity is for people who are un-righteous, who are willing to confront the reality of their separation from God, who are willing to step forward and say, "I'm guilty. I have no right to enter your kingdom. But I have received your forgiveness. I've repented of sin, and by your grace I've been made clean." With that, the Judge declares your case dismissed and welcomes you.

Donald Grey Barnhouse, when nineteen years old, preached for a week of special meetings in a small church in California. There were about two hundred people pres-ent each evening. There was a movement toward God in which many people professed to accept Christ as their personal Savior. On the fourth evening, a woman in her sixties came to the young preacher requesting a private interview. He asked her about her spiritual state. Finally, she said, "I have a great burden of conscience, and I decided after hearing you preach these four evenings that I would make my confession to you, no matter what the consequence."

He expected to hear some simple story of a difficulty that would be met most simply from the Word of God. Instead, he was astounded to hear her say, "Thirty-eight years ago, I murdered a man." Then, as though the confes-sion had taken a great burden from her shoulders, she told the details. Here, a woman, respectable, a pillar in that California town, unbeknownst to everybody else in that town, had murdered a man. When she was twenty-two, she lived in a boarding house in an Eastern city. A man who lodged on the same floor had wronged her and brought her to a point of terrible fear. One night he went to his room drunk and fell on the bed in a stupor. She entered his room and turned on the gas in the small heater without lighting it. She pulled the rug close to the door and closed it. She went to her own room and lay sleepless through the night until the alarm was given. Someone knocked on her door and told her that their fellow boarder had committed suicide. That was all there was to it. Her part in the murder was never detected.

She soon left the city, went to the West Coast, and began a new life. In the eyes of all her fellow citizens, she was highly respected and lived a life that was above reproach. Her crime had gone undetected by man. But she knew that what she had done was not hidden from God. She had become increasingly aware, under the preaching of the Gospel, that she had to meet God. She had learned that the sin which she had carried for thirty-eight years could be transferred to the Lord Jesus Christ. She could rest quietly in the work He accomplished in shedding His blood for the remission of sin.

Ten years later, a friend told Dr. Barnhouse about this woman's death, saying that she had borne a splendid Christian testimony during her closing years. She had often spoke of having been born again during the meetings at which Dr. Barnhouse had spoken. She had followed the advice to speak of the matter to no person. The sin was cast behind God's back and remembered against her no more, because she had come face-to-face with the God before whom no sin is hidden, before whom no iniquity can be covered.

Do you carry a hidden sin that would shock your loved ones? Or do you have the buildup of the sludge of self-righteousness in which you can build yourself up at the expense of others? You can be set free as you confront your accountability and turn your burden over to the Lord.

Self-confrontation is the key. Only as you are willing to admit your helplessness and make confession a regular and prayerful habit will you be able to draw upon the healing power of the forgiveness Christ offers.

The Ultimate Human Condition 4

Now we know that whatever the law says it speaks to those who are under the law, so that every mouth may be stopped, and the whole world may be held accountable to God. For no human being will be justified in his sight by works of the law, since through the law comes knowledge of sin (Romans 3:19-20).

THE APOSTLE Paul has described how the pagan, lost in his sin, needs to hear of the Gospel of Jesus Christ. Paul has shown us how the good person, the self-made man, the moralist, needs the Gospel. Now he tackles the most difficult issue of all. He deals with people like himself—Jews. Do they need the Gospel? After all, didn't God reveal Himself through the Jews? Aren't they the very highest of religious expression? Paul deals with this matter confrontationally.

In Romans 2:17 — 3:20, he describes the ultimate human condition in terms of traditional religion, twisted privilege, and the total depravity of the human race.

He's now coming to the end of his introductory argument. He knows that you and I must hear "the next to last word" before we confront in all its beauty "the last word." Paul takes the naiveté that marks our contemporary approach to questions of ultimate importance, and he confronts us with some stark realities. He presents three basic facts that describe the ultimate human condition.

I

Fact one. Traditional religion will ultimately leave you empty.

Let's take a look at the ultimate expression of traditional religion, with all its pluses and minuses. It's Judaism. "But I am a good Jew!" declares the Pharisee, the Saducee, and the Scribe. For years, Paul lived that way himself. He was proud of his accomplishments. In his letter to the Philippians, he talks about having "reason for confidence in the flesh." In fact, he makes a comparison of himself with other good religious people. If anyone else has reason for confidence in the flesh, Paul is convinced that he has more. After all, he was circumcised on the eighth day. He was an Israelite. He was part of the tribe of Benjamin. He was a Hebrew, born of Hebrews. He was a zealous persecutor of the church. He would not tolerate heresy against Judaism.

After coming to faith in Christ, Paul reflected on his previous religiosity. He had come to some conclusions. One of the more perceptive was that the traditionally religious person digs a hole for himself. There's a major difference between being religious and being a Christian — a fact a lot of people have never discovered. Fritz Ridenour has written a little paperback commentary on the book of Romans, titled *How to Be a Christian Without Being Religious*. On its cover it shows an impish little character with a brightly polished halo over his head. In one hand he's holding his "good guy" button. In his other hand he's cradling his "good deed diary." Pretty disgusting picture, isn't it?

Isn't there something stuffy and repulsive about "religious people?" You can feel them walking toward you. They have all the answers. They give the impression that their lives are well put together. In some cases, they are. They say the right things and do the right things. Everyday, they add a bit more polish to their halos. In the process, they give the impression that what they are actually practicing is Christianity. Far from it. Whatever the religion may be, the halo polishing syndrome is a negation of ultimate spiritual reality.

Every religion has its traditions. Some of them continue
to have spiritual significance. Yet there is built into religious expression a tendency to take what was once alive
and make a lifeless, cold tradition out of it.

One of my favorite musicals is *Fiddler on the Roof.* We
know it as the story of a Russian-Jewish family. The
father, Tevye, sings a whimsical song describing the traditions that have evolved in Judaism. The words go like this:

A fiddler on the roof.
Sounds crazy, no?
That I can tell you in one word —
Tradition!
Tradition, tradition, tradition.
Tradition, tradition, tradition.
Because of our traditions…and what
God expects him to do.

Who, day and night must scramble
     for a living,
Feed a wife and children,
Say his daily prayers?
And who has the right
As master of the house
To have the final word at home?
The papa, the papa — tradition.
The papa, the papa — tradition.

Who must know the way to make
     a proper home,
A quiet home, a kosher home?
Who must raise a family and
     run the home
So papa's free to read the holy book?
The mama, the mama — tradition.
The mama, the mama — tradition.

At three I started Hebrew school,
At ten I learned a trade.
I hear they picked a bride for me,
I hope she's pretty.
The sons, the sons — tradition.
The sons, the sons — tradition.

And who does mama teach to mend
   and tend and fix —
Preparing me to marry
Whoever papa picks?
The daughters, the daughters — tradition.
The daughters, the daughters — tradition.

This song captures the whimsy and cultural value of many of our traditions. However, when you allow your spiritual expressions to become calcified into tradition, you're in trouble. The religious traditionalist is one who puts his confidence in the containers of truth, not in the Person of God who is the ultimate truth.

Paul hits this head-on, reflecting about the Jewish traditions. The good Pharisee, Saducee, or Scribe, the religious Jew of Paul's day, put his confidence in three of these traditional expressions.

One, he counted on his name to save him. "But if you call yourself a Jew..." (Romans 2: 17). The religious traditionalist takes pride in his name, while at the same time keeping the personal relationship with God at a distance. I am a "Jew." I am a "Presbyterian." I am an "evangelical Christian." I am "Spirit-filled."

Two, the religious traditionalist relies on his Scriptures and thinks because he has studied them he automatically is in right relationship with God. The Jew had the law. He boasted about the law. He tended to put his confidence in the Torah, the book from God. Paul rhetorically refers to the Jew who relies upon the law and boasts about it, who takes pride in the fact he's instructed in it.

Three, the religious traditionalist is proud of his works. Paul refers to circumcision. He says, "Circumcision indeed is of value if you obey the law; but if you break the law, your circumcision becomes uncircumcision" (Romans 2:25). There's that pride of works. I faithfully participate in the sacraments. Look at what I do. I evangelize. I am active in social work.

Again, all of the above activities and all of these outward signs have a value to them as long as they do not become the beginning and the end of your expression of faith. If it's tradition, for tradition's sake, spiritual life is squeezed out and emptiness results.

The religious traditionalist is a proud person. Built into his self-image is an attitude of superiority. We can see the ultimate expression of this in Romans 2: 19-20. Paul accuses the religious traditionalist of seeing himself as "a guide to the blind, a light to those who are in darkness, a corrector of the foolish, a teacher of children, having in the law the embodiment of knowledge and truth."

Then Paul shifts gears, smoothly. He kind of smirkingly raises the question, "Aren't you great? Look at the traditions in which you boast. 'We have the great music of the faith. We're not too emotional. We have an ordered worship service. We put a stress on scholarship. We have a social concern. Tradition, tradition, tradition!'"

Is there anything wrong with these? Not a thing. It's only when they become the objects of our faith, the elements in which we place our pride, that they become empty. We can hold high the Book, bear the right label, and pray loud and long in public. But if that's all our faith is, then we are in bondage.

As if he hadn't sliced deeply enough, Paul then adds these rhetorical questions: "You then who teach others, will you not teach yourself? While you preach against stealing, do you steal? You who say that one must not commit adultery, do you commit adultery? You who abhor idols, do you rob temples? You who boast in the law, do you dishonor God by breaking the law? For, as it is written, 'The name of God is blasphemed among the Gentiles because of you'" (Romans 2: 21-24).

God does not condone self-styled, stuffy, religious traditionalists. You don't condone them either. Paul points out that the pagan can see right through them. He knows whether there's a genuine quality to the faith or whether one is simply going through a memorized routine. He can tell whether you or I are simply proud bearers of a name, a book, and some rituals, or whether we are related personally to God in Jesus Christ. Is the wedding band I wear my marriage? No. It's a symbol that says I'm married. It has tremendous significance to me. What would you think of a man who wears his wedding band as he climbs into bed with a woman other than his wife. The very symbol that has such depth of meaning becomes a sneer, a mockery.

These externals of our religious tradition can be hollow symbols or reflectors of something much deeper. The name Christian can reflect a humble quality of life in which I acknowledge my sin, my need of a Savior. By my very attitude of life I step forward and say, "My name is John. I'm a sinner. I need the help of Jesus Christ. I need your help. I've repented of sin. I am a Christian."

We can be persons of the Book, encountering the Living Word, Jesus Christ, through the written Word. The external rituals of the faith, such as the sacraments, can become an inward circumcision. Paul states it, "He is a Jew who is one inwardly, and real circumcision is a matter of the heart, spiritual and not literal. His praise is not from men but from God" (Romans 2:29). The completed Jew or the completed Gentile is one to whom Jesus has become a matter of the heart. The externals are only symbols of God's inner work of grace.

II

Fact two. Privilege is important as long as it doesn't become twisted.

You mean that being a good Jew counts for nothing? Do you mean that being a good faithful Presbyterian or Methodist or Lutheran doesn't amount to anything? Yes, it means a lot. You are privileged, as long as that privilege does not become twisted. You are privileged in that you have been entrusted with the truth.

"Then what advantage has the Jew? Or what is the value of circumcision? Much in every way. To begin with, the Jews are entrusted with the oracles of God" (Romans 3: 1-2).

It was to the Jews that the Messianic prophecies were made. It was to the Jews that God's future plans were revealed. It was to the Jews that God promised to bring blessing to the world. And those of us who have been entrusted with the continuity of the faith revealed have the responsibility to treat it wisely, and not distort it. We're not to play around with trivia, allowing the faith "once delivered to the saints" to become a calcified, rigid, dogmatic badge of exclusivity.

We've been given good news of how men and women can be set free from sin. We've been given the knowledge of what God did through Christ's death and resurrection. We have the privilege of pointing to the cross of Jesus Christ, the only bridge to life for every human being who walks the face of the earth.

We Christians have an amazing way of sitting around trying to count how many angels can stand on the head of a pin. It's a convenient avoidance to the confrontation of our sinful nature. We have the Good News. What do we do with it? Do we share it with our neighbors? Do they have any idea where we go on Sunday morning? Do they see any change in our lives as a result of the faith we claim to practice? You and I are privileged. Privilege means a lot, as long as we don't allow it to become a selfish, vested interest, but instead see it as something we have been called to give away to a world in need.

Paul raises another rhetorical question. What if some of us were unfaithful? Does it change God's faithfulness? Does it cancel out the impact of what He's done? Absolutely not. No matter how many persons rebel against God, He is still faithful to those who move past sterile religion to honest repentance and trust in Jesus Christ.

"[But] what if some were unfaithful? Does their faithlessness nullify the faithfulness of God? By no means! Let God be true though every man be false, as it is written, 'That thou mayest be justified in the words, and prevail when thou art judged'" (Romans 3: 3-4).

It's important to realize the Old Testament source of this passage. It is taken from Psalm 51:4. Paul quotes this psalm, giving an immediate flashback to King David. For one whole year, the king of Israel had tried to cover up his sins of adultery, murder, and hypocrisy, until the prophet Nathan had the strength of character to come, point a finger in his face, and say, "Thou art the man." Under the conviction of the Holy Spirit, David cries out for the mercy of God. He pleads:

Have mercy on me, O God, according to thy steadfast love; according to thy abundant mercy blot out my transgressions. Wash me thoroughly from my iniquity, and cleanse me from my sin!

For I know my transgressions, and my sin is ever before me. Against thee, thee only, have I sinned, and done that which is evil in thy sight, so that thou art justified in thy sentence blameless in thy judgment (Psalm 51: 1-4).

Paul then puts forward another rhetorical question. "If my sin highlights the righteousness of God, if it points out His truth and glory and grace, why don't I sin all the more, so that more glory can come to Him?" There's always that tendency among humans to search for the loophole or that little crevice we can crawl through. Wherever the Gospel of Jesus Christ is preached, there are those who will pervert it. They'll say if salvation is not by works, then works don't make any difference. Then go ahead and do as you please. Theologians have called this the "Antinomian Heresy." Probably a better way of putting it is that it's just a rationalization for sinful behavior. To talk about going out and sinning more so more glory can come to God because His grace seems all the greater is like inflicting the entire population of a large city with a highly contagious and dangerous disease so as to show off the curative powers of a new wonder drug.

Our wickedness serves to show the justice of God. This does not mean that God is unjust to inflict his wrath upon us. His condemnation is just. I have no excuse.

III

Fact three. There is a doctrine of the total depravity of man.

Paul's argument now comes to its climax. He says that the Gentiles have sinned against the light of nature and conscience. The Jews have sinned in defiance of the re-vealed law. Therefore, the whole world stands con-demned. None of us is morally superior and acceptable to God, not even the religious Jew. "What then? Are we Jews any better off? No, not at all; for I have already charged that all men, both Jews and Greeks, are under the power of sin" (Romans 3:9).

Then Paul goes on to give some proof texts from the Old Testament. He states, "None is righteous, no not one." He

talks about all having turned aside, all of us having gone
wrong. He talks about our throat being an open grave, full
of death. He talks about us using our tongues to deceive.
He talks about us having feet that are swift to shed blood.
He talks about our paths being ruin and misery. He talks
about us having no fear of God. Then he states the ultimate: "Now we know that whatever the law says it speaks
to those who are under the law, so that every mouth may
be stopped, and the whole world may be held accountable
to God. For no human being will be justified in his sight by
works of the law, since through the law comes knowledge
of sin" (Romans 3: 19-20).

This means that we're all in this together, from the least
religious person to the most religious person. The doctrine
of total depravity doesn't mean that every person is as bad
as he can be. There are many persons who are compara-
tively good. It's that every one of us is as bad off as he can
be.

The final argument is in. The law has done its work. It
has silenced anyone who might endeavor to declare his
own innocence. The law has pointed out that the whole
human race should be in the position of owing to God the
penalty of its transgressions. The bottom line is that you
and I are accountable to God. Every one of us is equal
before Him.

There is a universal need for righteousness that only
God can provide. The law was never designed to save men
or deliver us from slavery and the guilt of sin. It was
designed to point us to Jesus Christ. It was designed to
clean off a mud-splattered mirror so that we could take a
look at our own mud-splattered faces and turn to the one
who can make us completely clean. Now and only now are
we prepared to confront the righteousness of God and His
provision for us through Christ.

You don't have to pretend perfection. You don't have to

be extra pious. You don't need to spend any time polishing your halo. You are God's person, accepted in Christ if you have received Him as Savior. He is your perfecter. As much as you are tempted and sometimes fall, you are still His new creation.

The Bottom Line 5

*Since all have sinned and fall short of the glory of
God, they are justified by his grace as a gift, through
the redemption which is in Christ Jesus, whom God
put forward as an expiation by his blood, to be
received by faith (Romans 3:23-25a).*

PAUL HAS SKETCHED for us the ultimate human
condition. It isn't very good. There's not one of us
who can avoid it. Our ultimate position before God is to be
measured before God's law. Disaster awaits every single
one of us. Paul reviews everything he's said to this point in
Romans 3:19-20:

Now we know that whatever the law says it speaks to
those who are under the law, so that every mouth may be
stopped, and the whole world may be held accountable to
God. For no human being will be justified in his sight by
works of the law, since through the law comes knowledge
of sin.

Remember the "next to the last word." This is it in
review. If this is all there is to the book of Romans, then up
to this point the book will have been a waste of time. If all
we have is the "next to last word," our only hope is in
ethical humanism, in which we try to come up with some
alternative way of doing business with each other.

Thank God this is only the next to the last word. We
come to a sudden shift in all that Paul is saying as he
addresses us in Romans 3:21 with the words:

But now the righteousness of God has been manifested
apart from the law, although the law and the prophets bear

47

witness to it, the righteousness of God through faith in Jesus Christ for all who believe. For there is no distinction; since all have sinned and fall short of the glory of God, they are justified by his grace as a gift, through the redemption which is in Christ Jesus, whom God put forward as an expiation by his blood, to be received by faith. This was to show God's righteousness, because in his divine forbearance he had passed over former sins; it was to prove at the present time that he himself is righteous and that he justifies him who has faith in Jesus (Romans 3:21-26).

We've come to the bottom line. We're now looking at the final word.

I

The theme of Romans is the righteousness of God. Righteousness in its purest sense means "worth." Righteousness involves being considered of value. It involves significance. It is used in the Pauline epistles in three ways. First, it refers to the ethical conduct demanded by the Mosaic law. Second, it refers to the salvation which is the gift of God through Christ. Third, it refers to the ethical conduct demanded of the Christian — those attitudes and actions specifically taught by Jesus.

The righteousness of God expresses itself in three primary manifestations. One is that God is righteousness. He is of ultimate worth. He is of ultimate value. He has, by His very nature, all perfection. Second, God demands righteousness of you and me. This is His nature. There's no way of Him getting around it. He cannot tolerate sin. Three, God provides righteousness for you and me — the bottom line.

Every heresy that has defaced the church involves one of these three manifestations of God. There are those who believe that because God is a God of love there can be no eternal punishment, no final dealing with sin. They deny the righteousness of God. There are many who think that God will let people get by on some kind of lower scale. If you and I are good enough He'll accept us. Christ's sacrifice, on the cross is not needed. Salvation comes through character, through rites and ceremonies, through church membership, through the ordinances of the sacraments of the church. All of these minimize the fact that God demands righteousness. There are those who believe that Jesus was merely a man and could not provide the substitutionary atonement for sinners. Others believe that Jesus is God and that salvation is a joint venture between Jesus and man. The individual is part of the process.

No — a resounding no! God is righteousness. God demands righteousness of us. God provides righteousness. This is what the Gospel is all about. The Gospel is the story of a righteousness God who transfers His righteousness to you and me through Jesus Christ, giving us maximum worth and ultimate significance.

II

The major question raised by the book of Romans is, "How do we get this significance?"

We don't get it on our own. Romans 3:23 levels us all, saying, "Since all have sinned and fall short of the glory of God." This includes the pagan, the moralist, the religionist.

We can't earn it through our obedience to the law. "For no human being will be justified in his sight by works of the law, since through the law comes knowledge of sin" (Romans 3:20).

How then can we have this significance, this worth?

Paul gives us three concepts, *justification, redemption,* and *expiation* to help us understand how God made available His transfer of righteousness. These concepts give us a glimpse. They are not complete in and of themselves.

Others will be introduced as the letter continues. In order to help you understand these three concepts better, here are some brief word pictures.

Picture one: A court of law. The word that triggers this picture is *justification*, which means "to set right." Paul says that you and I are "justified by his grace as a gift" (Romans 3:24).

It happens time after time in our courts. A person goes on trial. The evidence is brought in. In some cases, the evidence proves the man is innocent. In other situations, there's not enough evidence to prove beyond a shadow of a doubt that he is guilty, and the defendant is acquitted.

This is not what justification is. The defendants (in this case you and me) happen to be guilty. Justification is the sovereign act of God in which He declares righteous the believing sinner while we are still in our sinning state. Some would say that justification is when the judge looks at the defendant as if he had never done any wrong. How many times have you heard that definition of justification, "just as if I had never sinned." No. Justification is when the defendant is clearly guilty. Yet God, in His amazing mercy, declares him innocent. He shares His righteousness with the person. He makes no rationalization for the defendant's wrongdoings but instead offers him an unconditional pardon. It's from that point that the defendant is treated as if he had never sinned. He is no longer guilty. The record is swept clean. He's a new man. The handcuffs are taken off. He starts life over again.

In its simplicity, the Gospel boils down to the simple phrase, "Jesus loves me! this I know, for the Bible tells me so." You and I are conscious of our sins. Penitent and brokenhearted, we come to God. Just as a good father forgives the prodigal, the wayward son, so God forgives the sinner who admits his guilt and claims the Lord's forgiveness. That's justification.

Picture two. This time it's a slave market. The word that

triggers this picture is redemption, which means to set free. The Bible says that you and I are "justified by his grace as a gift, through the redemption which is in Christ Jesus" (Romans 3:24). It's a scene out of the Roman slave market. There were some 600,000 slaves in Rome when Paul wrote this letter. Or, it's a picture straight out of one of the saddest chapters of American history. Picture the slave there on the auction block, stripped of all his clothing, humiliated in front of the crowd. The slave is owned by a vicious, hateful person who has dominated and humiliated him. Slaves come in all sizes, all shapes, all ages. Some are nubile. Some are strong and handsome. Some have been broken through beatings. Some go for a high price, some go for a small. Yet the owner treats all these persons as objects and ultimately will destroy them. They're only the means to his end. He holds them hostage. Suddenly, someone comes forward, walks resolutely to the auction block, reaches out his work-scarred hands, and says, "Come with me. I've redeemed you. You are ransomed. You are liberated." This is what Christ has done for us. Christ, fully God, fully man, has offered Himself as ransom to set you free from Satan's slavery. That's redemption.

Picture three. It is the temple. The word that triggers this picture is expiation, which means to take the place of. You and I who have sinned and fallen short of the glory of God "are justified by his grace as a gift through the redemption which is in Christ Jesus whom God put forward as an expiation by His blood to be received by faith." You and I immediately identify with the law court picture because of recent television series such as *Roots* and the incarceration of the hostages in Tehran. We can understand a bit of what it is to be purchased, to be redeemed from bondage. But this whole concept of sacrifice, of propitiation, of expiation is hard for us to handle.

In Old Testament times, if a man sinned, that sin put him

at once in wrong relationship with God. To get back in right relationship, he offered a sacrifice, usually a certain kind of an animal. Without the shedding of blood there was no remission for sin. And yet, those same Scriptures pointed out the need for the perfect sacrifice. The prophet, Micah, questioned whether the Lord would ultimately be pleased with the blood of thousands of rams. He wanted to know how he could really come before the Lord and have right relationship. The prophet Isaiah gave a hint as he yearned for the advent of the perfect lamb, prophesying that One would come who would be wounded for our transgressions, bruised for our iniquities. It's a new day. Christ is the Lamb of God whose blood covers us, washes us, makes us clean. He provides the repayment that we can never make.

This is expiation.

III

This sounds great, doesn't it? Do you mean I can really have this? How do I receive it?

You receive it by being fully convinced that God is able to do what He has promised — by faith. The way to right relationship with God is not through a frenzied, desperate, human effort, but by humble repentance and acceptance of God's gift purchased on the cross. Simple trust, simple faith.

Paul now directs three questions to you.

One is, what becomes of our boasting? He answers, "It is excluded." If we add up our works maybe we could boast just a little bit. But that's not the case. Our justification is by faith, not by works. Therefore, we stand very humble, with no room to boast, brag, or puff ourselves out of proportion.

Another question. Is God the God of the Jews only? Or is God the God of the Presbyterians only? Again, the answer is straightforward. God is the God of all creation. He will justify the circumcised Jew on the ground of his faith. He will justify the uncircumcised Gentile on the ground of his faith. Forget your label. God's not interested in what you call yourself or what you've done. He's given you a gift. Quit comparing yourself to everyone else. Accept the gift and then go out and tell other people about it.

A final question. Does that mean we should forget the law? Again, a straightforward, simple answer. "By no means! On the contrary, we uphold the law" (Romans 3:31).

Wait a second. You just told us we were free from the law. It's by faith; it's a free gift. That's right. But if we've been set free from bondage of the law, we're now set free to live within the liberating limits set by God's love. For through His Word, He's shown us a better way to live. I don't support my family because the law says a husband and father must support his family. I work hard, I share with them materially, emotionally, and spiritually because I love them. I don't avoid sleeping with other women for fear of venereal disease, or loss of job or reputation if I'm caught. I remain faithful to my wife, subordinating any other desires I might have, because of love, trust, and faithfulness, knowing that any temporary inconvenience or lack of pleasure is worth it for the ultimate value of being in right relationship with my wife. God, who has set us free by Christ's action on the cross, has shared with us how to live the wise way. He's not abolished the law. He has fulfilled the law.

I am convinced, after many years of Bible study, that these verses are the most important in the whole Bible. Understand them, and you will understand the whole Bible. Fail to comprehend their true meaning and you will be in darkness concerning most of the Scriptures. It is here that we see the revelation of God's righteousness and the infinite demands and provisions of that righteousness. It is here that we see sin for what it is. It is here that we find our ultimate hope and our very reason for being the church of Jesus Christ.

Donald Grey Barnhouse, in his multi-volume series on the book of Romans, says that early in his ministry he drew a heart next to the passage we have been discussing in this chapter — "I had drawn a heart; and I said that this passage was not only the heart of Romans, but the heart of the New Testament and the heart of the whole Bible."

These verses, I'm convinced, are the most important in all Scripture. Understand them and you will have a firm foundation upon which to rest your faith. Fail to comprehend them and you will be in darkness concerning most of the Bible. It is here that we see the revelation of God's righteousness and the infinite demands and provisions of that righteousness. It is here that we see sin for what it is.

It is here that we find our ultimate hope and our very reason for being the people of God.

A Case Study of Faith — Abraham   6

No distrust made him waver concerning the promise of God, but he grew strong in his faith as he gave glory to God, fully convinced that God was able to do what he had promised (Romans 4:20-21).

THE APOSTLE PAUL has just declared the most important truth to be found in the Bible. It answers one of the deepest yearnings of humanity. It's the question, "How can I be made right? How can I be whole? How can I be complete? How can I be what I was meant to be?"

In chapter 3 of Romans, the apostle Paul talks about the righteousness of God, equating it with the method by which you and I can be reconciled to God. He's talking about God's provision for us. He describes the way of righteousness by noting four particular characteristics.

First, the way of righteousness is apart from the law. Religion that is based on a code of action can easily become twisted into legalism and merit-seeking. There is nothing that stifles religion more than this life-consuming endeavor to pin merit badges on one's uniform to prove that you deserve the favor of God. A moral dynamic is needed which can break you free from this egocentric world. It's impossible for you and me to attain that requirement of obedience to God demanded by the law. Something more is needed than our own human effort. That effort, as beautiful as it is, becomes self-defeating.

Second, although the way of righteousness is apart from the law, it is attested to by the law. This is what Paul is saying in Romans 3:21 when he writes, "But now the righteousness of God has been manifested apart from the law, although the law and the prophets bear witness to it." What seems to be a radically new message has its roots in the Old Testament Scriptures. The Old Testament Scriptures were made up of three specific sections. There was the *Law,* the *Prophets*, and the *Writings*. Paul quotes from the Writings in Romans 3:10-18, describing from the Old Testament Scriptures that there is no one who is righteous. All have sinned. He then mentions in verse 21 that the Law and the Prophets also attest to this. Faith is nothing new at all. Salvation never has been of works. Faith was important before God gave the Law to Moses. Faith was important during the age of the Law. And, now, faith is essential in what we could call the Messianic Age, the era in which we now live.

Third, God's righteousness is provided in Christ through faith. Christ has perfected the atonement. Our imaginations have been triggered by three large theological words. *Justification* drew us into the law court where we saw a guilty defendant pardoned, swept clean. *Redemption* placed us in the slave market. There we saw a redeemer step forward, setting us free from our bondage to Satan. *Expiation* drew us to the holiest of holies, where the blood of the Perfect Lamb was offered as the supreme sacrifice for us, in our place as substitute for the penalty that technically should be ours.

Fourth, the righteousness of God is divinely just. Not only is God just, but God can justify us. Apart from Christ there is no justification. God is not being sidestepped. God is not a soft divine being who, in His sentimentality, takes our sin lightly. The price has been paid. Justice has been rendered, and you and I have been set free.

Could you ask for anything more difficult to understand? That's a lot of heavy, cognitive data. But the apostle Paul was basically a good teacher. He had a tremendous mind which could walk circles around the best scholars. He knew, however, that this heavy theology needed to be lightened by illustration. He declared, "For we hold that a man is justified by faith apart from works of law" (Romans 3:28). Then comes a shifting of gears as Paul moves from heavy, cognitive discourse into a practical case study of a person familiar to all who would read his letter. It was a case study showing how salvation is not of works but of faith.

Paul knew that a sermon or lecture is a house. Illustrations are the windows that let the light into the house. So, he takes Abraham as a case example. At this point he uses the Harvard Business School case study method to illustrate everything he's been trying to say in the first three chapters. He devotes the entire fourth chapter to a discussion of the faith and the character of Abraham. He makes three major statements about Abraham and then backs them up from Abraham's experience.

Statement One. *Abraham was justified by faith, not works.*

What a radical thought. Imagine what your response would be if you were Jewish. You mean to say that our forefather, Abraham, was not justified by his good works? Abraham was the perfect Jew. Isn't he our model? That's right, Paul says. Abraham is the model. You want to know how to be justified, how to be right before God? Look at Abraham. Abraham didn't do it by his good works. He was made right with God by his willingness to take God at His word. "For if Abraham was justified by his works, he has something to boast about, but not before God. For what does the scripture say? 'Abraham believed God, and it was reckoned to him as righteousness'" (Romans 4: 2-3).

Abraham, the father of the Jews, didn't earn his way

into God's favor. No. Abraham was a man of consummate humility who refused to boast. His life was commendable. He was a good example. What singled him out so specially before was his simple trust of God. Paul quotes Genesis 15:6, which reads, "Abraham believed God, and it was reckoned to him as righteousness." Abraham didn't purchase his righteousness. It was a gift of God freely accepted.

Paul then uses King David as an additional illustration. He cries out to God, grateful for His forgiveness. He's experienced what it is to receive salvation through faith, not through works. "So also David pronounces a blessing upon the man to whom God reckons righteousness apart from works: 'Blessed are those whose iniquities are forgiven, and whose sins are covered; blessed is the man against whom the Lord will not reckon his sin'" (Romans 4:6-8). This is a quotation from Psalm 31. David knows what it is to confront the righteousness of God, to realize that God demands righteousness of him. And, he knows what it is to experience the righteousness which God has provided, not because of David's good works. He had failed in that department. Instead, he had humbled himself and received salvation, had received the gift of righteousness.

One day I was invited to play golf with a good friend at his exclusive, private country club. The day before, I cashed a check at the bank to make sure that I had enough money to cover any expenses. I went into the pro shop to buy a package of balls and a glove. I held a twenty dollar bill in my hand. The man behind me, said, "Your money is no good here." There was no way that I could pay for those balls, gloves, the greens fee, and the lunch. I was a guest. I had the money. I could afford it. The fact was that my money was no good at that club. I had to depend on the hospitality of my host.

Your good works are important. They're simply not the currency of salvation. You are fully dependent upon your Host to pay the bill. You're called on to humbly receive a gift. Put your wallet back into your pocket.

Organized religion, whether it be Judaism or Christianity, has a way of perverting itself. You look at the counter and see salvation displayed. You know that you need a right relationship with God. You reach for your wallet, thinking that you can buy it, you can earn it, you can pay for it, only to confront God, who says, "Your money's no good here. Be my guest."

Statement Two. Abraham's circumcision was simply a sign of righteousness.

This was a radical concept to the Jews. They prided themselves in their circumcision. Today we don't talk much about circumcision. It's a minor surgical process done primarily for hygienic reasons. That's not what it meant to the Jews, however. A male baby was to be circumcised on the eighth day after his birth. This was a mark of his Jewishness. There were those who said a person could not be in fellowship with God unless he was circumcised.

What is there about being religious that causes us to attach ultimate significance to the symbols of our faith? Paul raises some questions. "Is this blessing pronounced only upon the circumcised, or also upon the uncircumcised? We say that faith was reckoned to Abraham as righteousness. How then was it reckoned to him? Was it before or after he had been circumcised?" (Romans 4:9-10).

He goes on to declare that the circumcision had nothing to do with his being reckoned righteous before God. Circumcision was a sign. It was the seal.

Two summers ago I lost a piece of luggage. The airline that lost it tried to track it down for three months. They finally admitted their failure. They asked me to reconstruct a list of everything in that suitcase, the date I bought it, and the price I paid for it. During the three-month period I had written down each of the items that must have been in the case as I discovered their absence. I wrote down to the best of my recollection what I had paid when I purchased them. Then I had to take that list to a notary public. The notary attested to the fact that I was swearing to be truthful. I could have lied. I could have pretended that there were some valuable jewelry items in that case, along with the tennis shoes, jogging shoes, dirty socks, underwear, and shirts.

Our religious rites, our baptism, our communion, are seals of an inner work of grace. The notary seal is not placed on a blank sheet of paper. It is placed there only as a sign that all that has been written on that sheet is attested to as correct by the one who wrote the document and signed his name on the dotted line. Abraham was not made right before God because he was circumcised. His circumcision was a sign that came quite a bit later. In obedience to God, it was a symbol of his trust in the Lord. Romans puts it in these words: "He received circumcision as a sign or seal of the righteousness which he had by faith while he was still uncircumcised. The purpose was to make him the father of all who believe without being circumcised and who thus have righteousness reckoned to them, and likewise the father of the circumcised who are not merely circumcised but also follow the example of the faith which our father Abraham had before he was circumcised" (Romans 4:11-12).

Let's not dupe ourselves into thinking that because we do good works, because we have all the outward signs of religious activity, that we have a right relationship with God. Our good works, our religious labels, our activities do not bring right relationship with God. They are important, yes. The true circumcision, though, is the circumcision of the heart, that inward work of God's grace which makes us clean, which makes us pure, which makes us righteous before Him.

Statement Three. There's a third lesson we learn in this case study of Abraham. Not only was Abraham justified by faith, not works. Not only was his circumcision simply a sign of righteousness, not the cause of righteousness. In addition, Abraham's God was big enough to truly be God.

Take a look at the life of Abraham. Yes, he accomplished many good works and he did some things wrong. His good works were the spin-offs of his right relationship with God which was based on faith. Abraham had confidence in the God to whom he entrusted his whole life. The author of Hebrews defines faith as "the assurance of things hoped for, the conviction of things not seen. For by it the men of old received divine approval. By faith we understand that the world was created by the word of God, so that what is seen was made out of things which do not appear" (Hebrews 11:1-3). The author goes on to tell us about Abraham, listing him among that great honor roll of faith, describing him as trusting the Creator-Sustainer God, who was not bound to the cultural limitations of any one group of people.

Young Abraham was raised in a pagan, idol-worshiping culture. In faith, he makes a break culturally with the idols of his father, and leaves the land of Haran believing that God had something better in store. He accepted the promises of God. He was a 75-year-old man when he took Sarah, his wife, and Lot, his nephew, and all their possessions, along with his servants, and headed for the land of Canaan. He lived in tents. He built altars for this God. He had to make decisions. He sought God's guidance on those decisions. He listened to the word of God and trusted that word as being reliable.

At times he must have thought he was crazy. Remember when he stood overlooking the fertile Jordan valley. He gave the choice of the land to Lot, his nephew, and Lot took the best plot of land. Abraham never complained about Lot's choice. God had given him many possessions and he realized that everything he had could be lost overnight. He was not a citizen of this world. His true citizenship was in heaven. His true sovereign was Jehovah. So what if Lot got the best land. Abraham would trust God.

Judged by works, you couldn't call Abraham righteous. He had misled Pharoah in Egypt. He had feared for his life and potentially compromised his wife. But he repented. He followed the Lord.

God had promised that Abraham would be the father of many nations. A cynic would scorn that promise. Abraham's wife laughed at the idea. "Abraham, how could you be the father of many nations when you haven't even got a son? You're childless. Not only that, I'm 90 years old and you're 100." How she laughed. What good reason he had to join her. A man his age and a woman hers don't have children.

But Abraham didn't laugh. His God was too big. Paul tells us that he hoped against hope. "He did not weaken in faith when he considered his own body, which was as good as dead because he was about 100 years old, or when he considered the barrenness of Sarah's womb. No distrust made him waver concerning the promise of God, but he grew strong in his faith as he gave glory to God, fully convinced that God was able to do what he had promised. That is why his faith was reckoned to him as righteousness" (Romans 4:19-22).

Then you remember how his son came — Isaac, the miracle child. Remember that testing of Abraham's faith as, in obedience to God, he took that child to Mount

Moriah. He was even willing to sacrifice his child of promise to God if God asked for it.

But God provided a substitute, and Abraham trusted in God's provision. Though he didn't fully understand, he stepped forward and believed.

How big is your God?

Robert Dick Wilson was one of the great professors at Princeton Theological Seminary. One of his students had been invited back to preach in Miller Chapel twelve years after his graduation. Old Dr. Wilson came in and sat down near the front. At the close of the meeting the old professor came up to his former student, cocked his head to one side in his characteristic way, extended his hand, and said, "If you come back again, I will not come to hear you preach. I only come once. I am glad that you are a big-godder. When my boys come back, I come to see if they are big-godders or little-godders, and then I know what their ministry will be." His former student asked him to explain, and he replied: "Well, some men have a little god, and they are always in trouble with him. He can't do any miracles. He can't take care of the inspiration and transmission of the Scripture to us. He doesn't intervene on behalf of his people. They have a little god and I call them little-godders. Then there are those who have a great God. He speaks and it is done. He commands and it stands fast. He knows how to show Himself strong on behalf of them that fear him. You have a great God; and He will bless your ministry." He paused a moment and smiled, and said, "God bless you," and turned, and walked out.

Abraham had a big God. I have a big God. You have a big God. Do you trust Him? Do you have faith in Him? Is your faith reckoned to you as righteousness?

Paul concludes his illustration from the life of Abraham with these words: "But the words, 'it was reckoned to him,' were written not for his sake alone, but for ours also.

It will be reckoned to us who believe in him that raised from the dead Jesus our Lord, who was put to death for our trespasses and raised for our justification" (Romans 4:23-25).

Read His word. Trust His atoning work through Jesus Christ. Listen to the quiet inner voice of His Holy Spirit and claim His righteousness provided for you. *Live* in the confidence that He will follow through on His promises, no matter how strange or beyond your understanding they may seem.

Since We Are Justified by Faith

7

Therefore, since we are justified by faith, we have peace with God through our Lord Jesus Christ. Through him we have obtained access to this grace in which we stand, and we rejoice in our hope of sharing the glory of God (Romans 5:1-2).

THE OTHER DAY I heard a very intelligent man state that he is a Christian. Someone asked him to define what he meant. He said, "A Christian is a good person, one who is considerate of other people. A Christian is loving. He lives as Christ lived."

Someone else asked if that was all there was to being a Christian. This person said, "You don't want to get too doctrinal and theological about these things, do you? Christianity really is an attitude."

What this man described was salvation by works. If there is a God, you can win his favor by following the example of Jesus, the best man who ever lived.

The Protestant Reformation stands for many things. Central to it is the cry: "The just shall live by faith!" The Bible speaks against salvation by works. You can't do enough of them to win salvation. Give gifts to religious causes, but don't think you can buy God's indulgence. Only your faith in Christ's atoning work will save you.

The apostle Paul opened his letter to the church at Rome with this strong affirmation, "The just shall live by faith" (Romans 1:17, KJV). He says it in so many different ways. Time after time he stresses justification by faith.

It's fascinating to know that Paul was so concerned about this biblical affirmation because there are other concepts about which he was somewhat indifferent. He refused to take too seriously the problem of meat offered to idols. He left that up to the individual conscience. He was quite casual about the observance of Jewish times and seasons. Even circumcision was allowed if it was not practiced in opposition to the Gospel. It was up to individual discretion whether or not it would be used or neglected.

However, he did not take the same relaxed view toward the doctrine of justification by faith. It was not optional. You either submit to it or perish. You can't substitute for it, or interfere with it to any degree, without making void the work of redemption.

The text for this chapter amplifies this theme.

Let's review the meaning of justification by faith.

What is it to be justified? What is it you do when you justify your checkbook? You take your bank statement together with your canceled checks. You arrange the checks in order. Then you compare those checks with those you've written down in your checkbook. You subtract from the bank balance any checks you've written which have not come through in canceled form. You add any deposits which do not show on that statement. And when you're done with all this calculation, you hope that the balance in your checkbook is identical with the bank balance. For most of us, that's pretty wishful thinking isn't it? Some of us have sat by the hour practically tearing out our hair trying to get our checkbooks justified.

What are we trying to do? We're trying to make right our accounts. There are those months when we breathe a sigh of relief. It all happens so easily, so smoothly. The bank's records and ours reconcile. Then there are those months when we have to go back through every check and deposit, redoing all of our arithmetic, trying to track down the error or remember that check we wrote which we forgot to record.

Justification means "Being made right." Today's English Version translates the text, "Now that we have been put right with God through faith." The Bible says that you and I are sinners and cannot justify ourselves. There's no way in which we can produce reasons to prove that we are right.

The Bible says that God justifies the sinner. By this it doesn't mean that He comes up with a list of reasons to prove that we are right. It doesn't even mean that He makes good people out of us. Justification means that God treats you and me just as if we had not been sinners at all. Although you and I could be brought to trial for our active and passive rebellion and be forever treated by God as criminals, God treats you and me as beloved children.

Let's push the checkbook analogy a bit further. One day you're trying to balance your checkbook. You've let it go for a long time. In your confusion you made mistakes of arithmetic. You've mortgaged all your holdings to gain cash for highly speculative investments. The investments failed. Suddenly the bank calls, confronting you with huge overdrafts. It is calling due the mortgages. There's no way you could ever repay the amount. All of your assets fall short. The bank can't forgive you. It can issue a consolidation loan and charge interest, but it can't forgive your indebtedness. There'll be examiners who'll check it out. You may even be a friend of the president, but there's no way he can manipulate the figures to let you off. You're bankrupt.

In your financial despair, you don't know which way to turn. But wait! Along comes a friend who loves you and is determined to help you. He identifies with you in your need and at a great sacrifice, writes a check to cover your indebtedness, justifying all your mistakes, bad investments, and errors, paying off your loans and bringing your checkbook into balance with the bank statement.

This is what God has done for you in Christ. You are

justified, set right. There's a difference between forgiveness and justification. Forgiveness is a relationship with God. It's personal. Justification is a status before God in which you are set right. The account is paid.

What then is the meaning of faith? The text says, "Therefore since we are justified by faith.... "

Faith is the total acceptance and absolute trust that Christ has made provision for your sins, making possible your right relationship with God. It's a reliance upon Him and His finished work in the full realization that there's nothing you can do to earn your salvation.

Faith is what a little child has in a parent when that child leaps from a high perch into the outstretched arms of a loving father. There's a difference. An uncoordinated father, with every good intent, could miss catching the child and thus injure him. Our trust is in a heavenly Father who will never let us slip through His arms.

Faith is reliance upon Jesus Christ and His finished work on the cross.

There is a fascinating movement within Romans 5:1-2. It comes alive in three simple words: "therefore" and "we have."

"Therefore" refers to the conclusive argument Paul has made throughout the first four chapters of Romans. It specifically relates to chapter four and the example of Abraham. Paul has gone to great lengths to show that you and I are called to have faith like that of Abraham. Abraham, too, was justified by faith, not the law. He had believed the promises of God even though there was no way he could touch and handle them.

The righteousness of Abraham and other Old Testament saints was not that they faithfully adhered to the Law. It was that they trusted in the God who had given them the Law and, as a result, were obedient to His commands. This is a revolutionary concept. We must remind ourselves of it time and time again.

Paul says that "therefore" since we, like Abraham, are justified by faith, not by works, "we have" three magnificent possessions. What are these possessions?

First. We have *peace* with God through our Lord Jesus Christ.

Whereas the Revised Standard Version reads, "We have peace with God through our Lord Jesus Christ," other ancient manuscripts read, "Let us have peace with God through our Lord Jesus Christ." Since you are justified by faith, you are given peace. This is a state of reconciliation as opposed to an enmity relationship. You're encouraged to enjoy this, to retain it, to continually experience this wholeness, this fullness, this restored relationship which is yours with God. This peace is a creative harmony with your total environment that is not dependent upon your environment being calm and placid. Philippians 4:7 tells us that this peace passes all your human understanding. It's a stability that mounts guard over your entire existence. Jesus in John 14:27 tells us that it's a peace the world cannot give. It's not just inward contentment. It's the wholeness that comes when alienation and estrangement are removed.

You know the feeling, don't you? You've injured a loved one. You've done something to that person and you feel so bad about it that you don't want to look him in the eyes. You don't want to see him. Finally, you go and apologize. You mean it. You're sincere. Sweeping over you is that tremendous relief which comes from restored relationship when that apology is accepted. That's the peace I'm talking about.

Hold on to it. Guard it. It can slip away from you if you do not nourish it, being in a constant faith relationship with Jesus Christ.

Second, We have *access* to the grace of God.

Paul put it in these words: "Through him we have obtained access by faith to this grace in which we stand."

Grace is not only the attitude that God has toward you, it's what He actually gives you through Christ's self-giving justifying act. You have access to God's unmerited favor. You are literally ushered into the presence of divine royalty.

I've only had the privilege of meeting one earthly king. It's very difficult to gain access to a king's presence. Try flying to London to see Queen Elizabeth. Unless you have the right credentials, it's impossible to gain access. You could stand in front of Buckingham Palace for the next several months, banging in the gates and still never get in. There are guards all around royalty. Yet if you have the right introduction, it's very simple.

It is Christ's unmerited favor, His grace, that allows us into the presence of Almighty God. Christ makes the appointment. He gives us a letter of introduction. He ushers us into the eternal presence of Almighty God on His authority, not on ours.

In the Greek, this word access not only implies your right to be ushered into the presence of royalty, it also conveys a picture of seamanship. You're at sea in the middle of a storm. A tumultuous ocean is taking its toll on you and your fellow passengers. Suddenly, you are escorted by another ship into the calm of a haven. You have access to the harbor's safety.

Third. We *rejoice* in our hope of sharing the glory of God.

This means that you and I have the privilege of boasting, exhalting in the future that will be ours as we will spend eternity sharing the glory of our God. We are exhorted to rejoice and to keep on enjoying our peace with God.

This is quite a change. The glory of our creation, character, and destiny has been lost through sin. We were created in the image of God. We were in his likeness. All that was lost. Now we are assured that it is being restored. In this hope we triumph. This restoration is still incomplete. We see through a glass darkly. We have not realized it in its fullness although eternal life begins now, in this life.

Paul pauses at this point. He's quick to admit that he's only experienced in the incompleteness of this ultimate glory. He's not about to be phony, to make false promises. He knows how much he's suffered in this life. He's suspicious that some day, he'll probably go to his death a martyr, so he adds these words:

> More than that, we rejoice in our suffering, knowing that suffering produces endurance, and endurance produces character, and character produces hope, and hope does not disappoint us, because God's love has been poured into our hearts through the Holy Spirit which has been given to us (Romans 5:3-5).

Even as Paul speaks of the joy that is ours as believers, he recalls his sufferings. Then he reminds himself that instead of destroying hope, they strengthen hope; as he has been tested and found full of faith.

Some of us have experienced the reality about which Paul writes. This isn't something that happened back 2000 years ago and can't happen today.

Let me tell you the story of one couple I know. It was back around 1970. A couple had called the Key Biscayne Presbyterian Church telling the secretary that they wanted to have their baby baptized. I made an appointment to visit them at home. My mind boggled as I walked into their magnificent, contemporary, waterside home. Tom, a handsome young man in his mid-thirties, walked me through the home out onto the dock where his captain was working on a 65-foot motor yacht. After a few minutes of pleasantries, Tom brought up the baptism matter.

Then, as now, I told him that we couldn't baptize just anyone. At least one of the parents had to be a professing believer in Jesus Christ. He was sort of startled, thinking that any little child could, and should, be baptized. Tom told me about churches to which he had belonged; although since his divorce and remarriage, he hadn't been too active anywhere. But he tried to live a good life.

I talked with him about the claims of Christ and what it means to be justified by faith, not good works. I asked him if he was willing to acknowledge the fact that he was a sinner and needed a Savior; if he was willing to put his trust, his faith, in the crucified and risen Christ. That was too much for Tom. I suggested postponing any talk about baptism until he was willing to come to grips with his own personal relationship with Jesus Christ until he could, with integrity, take the vows that would be his as a parent. I expressed my availability at any time to talk with him about spiritual matters. Then we walked into the house. He somewhat awkwardly tried to explain to his wife that Juliette could not be baptized now. I left wondering if I'd ever see Tom and Bea again.

During the next few months, they would occasionally show up in church. Then, much to my surprise, Anne and I received an invitation to have dinner with them at their home. We arrived, were met at the front door, ushered through their central, tropical garden into the living area of the house, and from there on out to their yacht. The captain started up the engines. Bea served us a gourmet meal, accompanied by casual conversation, as we cruised in Biscayne Bay. As we lingered over dessert, the conversation shifted. For the longest time, Tom and Bea peppered us with questions about the Christian faith. Then they excused themselves, saying they needed to go below for a few minutes to talk something over. Anne and I couldn't figure out what was going on.

A few minutes later, they emerged from below to announce, "We've made our decision. We want to become Christians." Could it be for real? Tom, who had made a fortune in the communications business, who had one broken marriage and a lifestyle that was anything but that of Christians we knew. Could they be serious? Together we bowed in prayer.

The months went by. They became active in the church. They went with us to the Holy Land and extended that trip to visit our missionaries in Kenya. Some years went by, and in 1973 I was called to serve First Presbyterian Church of Pittsburgh, Pennsylvania.

Tom had always dreamed of sailing the ocean. He sold his business and after one abortive attempt on the motor yacht, sold the boat and had a sailboat built to his specifications. Four years ago, he, Bea, and their daughter sailed the Atlantic. They went down the coast of Europe into the Mediterranean, down the coast of Africa, back across the south Atlantic, up the coast of South America to the Caribbean, and back up the North American coast.

Four years ago, I looked out into the sanctuary on World-Wide Communion Sunday. Who was sitting a few rows back? Tom and Bea. We embraced after church. They were anchored in Annapolis, Maryland, and had driven over for church on Sunday. As we had dinner together, they told about how God had been working in their lives in recent years. Then Tom told of his vision, "You know, money just doesn't mean a whole lot anymore. I don't have nearly as much as I used to, but then I don't really care because Bea and I would like to go into full-time Christian missionary work. We want your counsel on how this can happen."

They checked with several mission organizations before joining the staff of Campus Crusade for Christ. They went through a thorough lay-training program. After short-term special project assignments in Southeast Asia and Europe, Tom and Bea Hingle are now living in a trailer in Newport Beach, California. Tom is back in the communications business, now as a "tent maker," using his expertise to make enough money to survive economically while helping Christian organizations such as Fuller Seminary, World Vision, and Campus Crusade cut their communications costs.

Justified by faith, this couple has been dramatically transformed by God's grace. You say, "Too dramatic. You're talking about pretty people, stories of affluence, fancy happenings." All I can say is that spotted all over the world today are examples of people who are experiencing the reality of what it is to be justified by faith, knowing this same peace, access to grace, and joy that God offers.

In this world of "do it yourself," "self-help," and the ceaseless striving after success, it's comforting to know that our salvation does not depend on our own efforts. Comforting, yes, but necessarily comfortable, no. The road to a living faith is filled with suffering. Paul has promised us this in Romans 5:3-5. But he has also promised us that through the suffering comes endurance, and through the endurance comes the hope "that does not disappoint us." Though the battle between our old and new natures will go on constantly, the Holy Spirit will continually make us aware that we need have no fear, no guilt. We have been set right with God — we are justified.

Positives Produced by Suffering 8

> *More than that, we rejoice in our sufferings, knowing*
> *that suffering produces endurance, and endurance*
> *produces character, and character produces hope,*
> *and hope does not disappoint us, because God's love*
> *has been poured into our hearts through the Holy*
> *Spirit which has been given to us (Romans 5:3-5).*

ONE OF THE PRIMARY strengths of the Christian faith is that through Jesus Christ you are equipped to face eternity. You understand that life does not end with death. You have a future beyond this life. Those who are saved, born again by the Spirit of God, are promised eternity in heaven with Jesus Christ. The apostle Paul declares this future hope. It is God's realistic promise to those of us who are justified by faith because of God's grace in Jesus Christ. "We rejoice in our hope of sharing the glory of God" (Romans 5:2).

But we need not limit our rejoicing to the promises of the future. You and I are privileged to rejoice now in this life no matter what our circumstances are. Paul puts it in these words: "More than that, we rejoice in our sufferings" (Romans 5:3).

I

The Christian life is ruggedly realistic in that it offers peace during suffering, not escape from suffering. Think about that. It's not a popular message. Many religious media personalities are huckstering Jesus on the false promises that Jesus will take away all your sufferings. Scripture, however, runs directly counter to this notion. It addresses the crude, tough realities of contemporary existence.

I'm not going to try to deal with this topic in its totality. The apostle Paul does not try to do that in the fifth chapter of Romans. In fact, I find that the biblical writers, inspired as they were by the Holy Spirit, didn't try to give all the answers. Read the book of Job. You see a godly man going through desperate suffering. His three well-meaning friends gather around and try to explain to him the reasons for his suffering. Some of their arguments are pretty impressive. But they are rebuked by God. As well-intentioned as they are, and as plausible as some of their arguments may be, they had embarked on an impossible task.

If God had wanted us to have all the answers, He would have clearly outlined them in the Scriptures. Beware of anyone who has simple answers to complex questions. Granted, every pastor who daily struggles with his own pain and the hurts of others will try to fit together that perfect mosaic which pictures the answers for all to see. Yet, in our most reflective, honest moments, we'll admit the edges are rough, and there are some empty spaces in the middle that we'll only understand when we are made perfect as we enter into the presence of the One who is perfect. In the meantime, we live in the real world. People suffer, people hurt, and more often than not we do not understand why. We continue to identify with our own hurts and the hurts of others as God gives us strength. We'll continue trying to find some symmetry to it all.

The text for this chapter, although not trying to fit it all together, gives us some insight as it shows us some of the positives produced by suffering.

The Bible alerts you and me to the fact that every one of us suffers in one way or another. One of Job's counselors states it so succinctly when he says, "For affliction does not come from the dust, nor does trouble sprout from the ground; but man is born to trouble as the sparks fly upward" (Job 5:6-7). The apostle Paul acknowledges suffering as he describes his own struggles. In 2 Corinthians, chapter 11, he describes his imprisonments, countless beatings, and narrow escapes from death. Five times he had received thirty-nine lashes. Three times he had been beaten with rods. Once he was stoned. Three times he had been shipwrecked. Many times in danger from rivers, thieves, robbers in cities and in wildernesses. His had been a life of toil and hardship. He'd spent many a sleepless night. He had been hungry. He had been thirsty. He had been exposed to cold.

He's not trying to tell you and me that if we come to Jesus all our problems will go away. He's echoing the constant refrain of all of the biblical writers — that both believers and nonbelievers will have trouble in this world. And sometimes those of us who are believers in Jesus Christ will have more immediate sufferings than those who are taking the easy way by living pleasure-oriented lives.

It is in this context of facing the reality of suffering that Paul paints a description of those of us who are believers, referring to us as persons who "rejoice in our sufferings."

The Latin word for suffering is *tribulare* out of which comes the word tribulation. It means "to press, to oppress, to afflict." It brings to mind a picture of the Roman tribulum, a threshing sledge that separated the grain from the chaff. It consisted of a wooden platform studded underneath with sharp flints or iron teeth. As this instrument passed over the pile of grain, the wheat was separated from the straw. You can well understand how a person undergoing affliction would compare his sufferings with those that would be inflicted if such an instrument passed over him. You mean that you and I, as believers, should rejoice in such cutting, grinding pressure?

The Greek word for tribulation carries the same terrible

thought, but with slightly different imagery. The word is *thlipsis*. It originally conveyed the idea of "pressing together, putting under pressure." The application of this word to human suffering was first employed in the New Testament. Christians were the first to think of themselves as being in a vat, like grapes or olives, and being pressed to the point where their joy ran out like wine or oil. Paul is telling us that our sufferings can press out of us joy as one presses wine from grapes or oil from olives.

There are many biblical references to oil and wine. Most of them are tied in with the theme of joy. Psalm 45:7 speaks of the "oil of gladness." Psalm 104:15 refers to "wine that maketh glad the heart of man."

Donald Grey Barnhouse had this to say about joy and suffering: "If you are to be splashed with joy, you must be crushed." Then he developed a logical thought progression in the analogy in which he showed how the olive and the grape became oil and wine.

To be a Christian is a wonderful gift of God. To be a Christian who wants to live an antiseptic existence is to yearn for something cheap, something less than the existence that can be yours if you realize that through the crushing process of suffering an even greater joy can be known.

The fullness of joy is for the olives and the grapes to be crushed. The great vineyards have their own secrets for making the most valuable wines. No, you and I are not to look for trouble. We're not supposed to create suffering for ourselves. But when the crushing comes we should not be surprised. Ours can be joy even through that difficult experience, knowing that God is sovereign.

I dare you to show me a Christian who has genuinely opened his life to the Lordship of Jesus Christ whose quality of life has not been enriched by suffering. Yet, it's sad to say, there are some of us who bear the name Christian who are doing everything we possibly can to protect ourselves from difficulty. We avoid suffering by refusing to reach out and get our hands dirty with the problems of others. We refuse to open our hearts to people who knowingly or unknowingly could hurt us badly. We live protectively, insulating ourselves off from the brokenness of others, and, in the process, minimize our own potential for wholeness. Don't talk to me about the nine million refugees. I don't want to hear about the boat people. Don't tell me about the Thai-Cambodian border. Don't describe what's happening on the edge of Afghanistan, where 400,000 refugees now tremble in the cold and attempt to find shelter in Pakistan after the Russian invasion of their homeland. By all means, don't tell me about Africa. I don't want to be reminded. Because then I feel guilty. I feel as though I should do something. It disturbs my complacency. I've got enough problems of my own at home.

"She has an alcohol problem. That's why I divorced her. She was making my life miserable. She was destroying the lives of our kids. She wasn't the same person I married."

"He never did meet my needs. I cleaned the house. I cooked for him. I bore him four children. All he did was spend his time at the office. I have every right to have a career also. I have the right to be happy. I'm going to do it my way. I'm going to have some fun for a change. He'll never hurt me again."

What's your version of this modern-day myth, "I have the right to be happy." It's one way in which we flee from intimacy. It's one way that we get around coping with reality. It's our excuse for breaking vows we've taken. We don't want to feel the pain. We've never learned that just beyond the pain there's a joy, perhaps the joy of finding an intimacy with another human being who has also built up his defenses as he cries out for someone to share the common frailties, the common hurts. Or, maybe that one will only grow harder and only hurt you more. Yours may be the joy of discovering dimensions within yourself you never knew you had as you remain faithful to the vows you've taken and expose yourself willingly to the hurts of others whose pain you can help lessen.

God is not only a God of a distant eternity. He functions in time right here, right now. "For thus says the high and lofty One who inhabits eternity, whose name is Holy: 'I dwell in the high and holy place, and also with him who is of a contrite and humble spirit, to revive the spirit of the humble, and to revive the heart of the contrite'" (Isaiah 57:15). You and I have the joy of knowing that we have a high priest named Jesus Christ who is "touched with the feeling of our infirmities." He has suffered in every way as we have suffered. And He will walk through our suffering with us.

II

Suffering has three positive functions.

First, your suffering may be God's corrective.

We're not talking about your making a payment for your sin. Jesus did that. No one else can pay the price for your sin but Him.

There are times in which you and I are headed down a wrong path. It may be that we have willfully disobeyed God. It may be that we have just stumbled onto a siding and have become confused. And God has placed a barrier right in the middle of our road.

Jeremiah knew the feeling as he spoke on behalf of his fellow Jews. He was boxed in with gloom. Jerusalem had been devastated by Nebuchadnezzar. The proud city had been destroyed. Jeremiah's friends had been taken captive. The once beautiful people had been left rotting in the streets. Infants lay there with parched tongues cleaving to the roofs of their mouths. Some persons were so hungry that they turned to cannibalism. Jeremiah cries out, "He has walled me about so that I cannot escape; he has put heavy chains on me; though I call and cry for help, he shuts out my prayer, he has blocked my ways with hewn stones, he has made my paths crooked" (Lamentations 3:7-9).

Then Jeremiah, after lamenting on and on about the desperate condition of his people and his own particular need, remembers that the grape when crushed turns into wine, the olive when crushed turns into oil. He writes these words of rejoicing: "But this I call to mind, and therefore I have hope: The steadfast love of the Lord never ceases, his mercies never come to an end; they are new every morning; great is thy faithfulness" (Lamentations 3:21-23).

God deals with you and me today even as He dealt with His people of the old covenant. There are times when He has to get our attention. He allows Satan access to our lives. He sees us as stiff-necked people. For some of us it takes suffering to catch our attention. We have to hit our heads up against the blockade in the road time after time until we come to our senses and turn around and go back to the main road where the Savior once again waits to escort us on to the celestial city.

Second, some suffering is constructive.

There are many analogies regarding affliction and suffering. There's the polishing of the arrow shaft. It's an abrasive process, but it makes it smooth. There's the chiseling process of the sculptor as he chips away at the crude granite. There's the potter who makes the vessel. You and I are vessels, being molded, perfected by the Master Craftsman. Isaiah's imagery is so vivid. Then there's Malachi, who describes the refining process. The white heat of the fire melts the silver, melts the gold.

Impurities are skimmed off the top. The heat is searing and painful, but the final product is much more precious as a result.

Third, there is that suffering which serves as an example to the glory of God.

It's not just the sinner who suffers. Believers suffer as well. In fact, sometimes it is the nonbeliever who prospers most.

What would the world think if every Christian had an easy life. You and I don't tend to relate to people who have everything going for them, do we? We tend to resent them because their lives are too easy. It's the person who has suffered who sets an example and reflects the glory of God.

That's what the story of Job is all about; God allowed Satan access to His servant. It's important to note that Satan could not do anything to Job that God would not allow him to do. God was sovereign. He could just as easily have turned Satan away. Even if God does allow the believer to come into difficult circumstances, He will not allow him to be tested above and beyond his abilities to withstand it. He is with the believer in it as he opens himself to God through the testing process. God will be faithful.

Remember that blind man from John 9:2? The question was raised as to whether he was blind because of his parents' sin. Or was it because of his own that he was born blind? Jesus dismisses the whole question. It is academic. He says that the man was born blind so that the works of God should be manifested.

Hosea. What a pathetic character. His wife was an adulteress, a harlot. She'd come home temporarily and then take off again. Each time he would welcome her back. Hosea was a model of forgiveness. He was God's person. His faithfulness has come down through the ages as a symbol to the faithfulness of Jesus Christ, for those of us who are His Bride, the church, who go whoring off in unfaithfulness to Him.

Paul puts it on the line. He says that suffering produces endurance. It helps us to be more patient. He says that suffering produces character. As you build your endurance, you mature. You're tested. You're disciplined. The rugged times prove the mettle in a person. They knock the whine out of you. They toughen you. Suffering produces hope. You get the rhythm of this? From endurance to character to hope.

I urge you to read a book titled *A Step Further*, written by Joni Eareckson. As a teenager, she had everything going for her until she dived into the Chesapeake Bay in the 1960s and, today, lives paralyzed from the neck down. In this book she describes her pilgrimage from a time when she was so desperate that she wanted to kill herself. Her thought-provoking words challenge us to think through our own sufferings. "Here I was, trapped in this canvas cocoon. I couldn't move anything except my head. Physically, I was little more than a corpse. I had no hope of ever walking again. How I prayed for some accident or miracle to kill me. The mental and spiritual anguish was as unbearable as the physical torture. But once again, there was no way for me to commit suicide. This frustration was also unbearable. I was despondent, but I was also angry because of my helplessness. How I wished for strength and control enough in my fingers to do something, anything, to end my life."

Now, over ten years later, she says that she can hardly remember how it was to feel that way:

Oh, I'm still paralyzed — still can't walk, still need to be bathed and dressed. But I'm no longer depressed. And to be honest, I can even say that I'm actually glad for the things which have happened to me.

Glad? How can that be? What has made the difference? My artwork and my supportive family and friends helped pull me out of my depression. But the heartfelt gratitude I have for this life in a wheelchair could only have come from God and his Word. They helped me piece together some of the puzzle which was so confusing. It took some seeking and studying. But today as I look back, I am convinced that the whole ordeal of my paralysis was inspired by his love. I wasn't a rat in a maze. I wasn't the brunt of some cruel divine joke. God has reasons behind my suffering, and learning some of them has made all the difference in the world. He has reasons for your suffering too.

A Study in Contrasts — The First and Second Adams

If, because of one man's trespass, death reigned through that one man, much more will those who receive the abundance of grace and the free gift of righteousness reign in life through the one man Jesus Christ (Romans 5:17).

ROMANS 1:1 through 3:20 describes the condemnation which is ours because of sin. Romans 3:21 through 5:21 emphasizes justification by faith, showing how we are freed from condemnation by what God has done for us in Jesus Christ. Romans 6:1 through 8:39 develops the doctrine of sanctification, showing how the Holy Spirit empowers those of us who are justified by faith to live lives of spiritual victory.

In this chapter I will discuss Romans 5:12-21. This passage marks Paul's transition from an emphasis on justification by faith to his teaching on sanctification. These verses serve as a bridge that will review some of what he has already told us, while adding some additional dimensions that will both agitate and stimulate.

I

The human race was specially created by God. It is not the result of some naturalistic evolutionary process in which man physically evolved from lower forms of life to what we now call Homo sapiens.

The Christian is one who believes the first chapters of Genesis. We do not try to make them say more than they say. We do not try to date the creation of man. We do not try to make the Bible primarily a textbook of science,

85

causing unnecessary conflict with anthropology and geology. But one fact is very clear. Nothing exists that did not come from God. In the very beginning God created the heavens and the earth. He created light, separating it from darkness. He created the planet Earth, separating the seas from the dry land. He placed vegetation upon this planet. He created animal life. He looked at all of His creation and He concluded "that it was good."

> But God saw that something was missing, and God said: Let us make man in our image, after our likeness; and let them have dominion over the fish of the sea, and over the birds of the air, and over the cattle, and over all the earth, and over every creeping thing that creeps upon the earth (Genesis 1:26).

In this first of the two creation accounts, Genesis records:

> So God created man in his own image, in the image of God he created him; male and female he created them (Genesis 1:27).

In the second of the two creation accounts we see a more specific account of God forming Adam out of the dust from the ground and breathing into his nostrils the breath of life. We see Adam's incompleteness. God causes a deep sleep to fall upon him. He takes one of his ribs, shaping from it Eve. The Bible tells us that Adam and Eve were both naked and were not ashamed.

God placed them in the garden. They were given dominion over all plant and animal life. They had everything going for them. They were His special creation. They were in the very image of God Himself.

Although the word, Adam, in the Hebrew can refer generically to mankind, this is not the use made by the biblical writers. They refer to Adam with specificity, as a literal human being. This fact is tremendously important as the apostle Paul, inspired by the Holy Spirit, continued to build an important Christian doctrine on the fact that there was a literal first man named Adam.

II

This passage explains the existence of sin in a way that eliminates some quaint but false understandings about where it came from.

The Bible teaches that sin existed before Adam in the person of Satan. This raises the question of where Satan came from. According to the Bible, God created all things and His creation was perfect. Not only did He create the universe, He also created innumerable spiritual beings, referred to in the Scriptures as angels, archangels, principalities, powers, seraphim, and cherubim, in ascending order of knowledge, power, and authority. At the head of creation, God placed the most splendid creature ever to come from His almighty hand. His name was Lucifer. Through the prophet Ezekiel, listen as God describes him as "the signet of perfection, full of wisdom and perfect in beauty" (Ezekiel 28:12). God goes on to describe this magnificent creature who became proud, rebelling against God, and who was thrown from his prestigious place, only to become the mortal enemy of God. He had wanted to be worshiped. He had wanted to be supreme. Sin began when Lucifer said:

> I will ascend to heaven; above the stars of God. I will set my throne on high; I will sit on the mount of assembly in the far north; I will ascend above the heights of the clouds, I will make myself like the Most High (Isaiah 14:13-14).

God describes something happening within Lucifer that took him from the very highest pinnacle of creation in which he served God to the point in which he vied with God for the highest honor. Ezekiel 28:15-16 reads:

> You were blameless in your ways from the day you were
> created till iniquity was found in you. In the abundance of
> your trade you were filled with violence, and you sinned;
> so I cast you as a profane thing from the mountain of God,
> and the guardian cherub drove you out from the midst of
> the stones of fire.

These verses present the key to the biblical doctrine of
original sin. It explains how sin erupted in the midst of a
sinless universe. Some Bible scholars go so far as to say
that there is a major gap between Genesis 1:1 and Genesis
1:2. They say that it was in this period that Lucifer fell and
the very existence of darkness that we see in verse two
proves the prior existence of sin and judgment.

This brings us back to Adam. Now we have the perfect
man and the perfect woman, created in the image of God
with the capacity to choose between right and wrong. We
see them as they are seduced by Satan, who promises
them that they can be like God Himself, a promise he
continues to whisper in our ears today. Adam and Eve
believe Satan, ignoring the one simple command of God:

> You may freely eat of every tree of the garden; but of the
> tree of knowledge of good and evil you shall not eat, for in
> the day that you eat of it you shall die (Genesis 2: 16-17).

They simply didn't believe God, and chose to disobey
him. Their action ushered sin into the world.

What I'm telling you is what the Bible says. It speaks
clearly of a literal Adam and Eve. It unequivocally states
that Adam's disobedience has implications for every human being. Because of Adam's sin, you and I are also
condemned, are lost, have fallen from the original intention that God had for the human race.

There are some other viewpoints on this doctrine. Wil-
liam Barclay notes that Paul says that all men sinned in
Adam. He goes on to say that if we are ever to understand
Paul's thoughts here, we must be quite sure that Paul

meant what he said. All through the history of Christian thinking there have been efforts to interpret this conception of the connection between Adam's sin and mankind in different ways.

One view says that the passage should be interpreted to mean that *"each man is his own Adam."* Just as Adam sinned, all the rest of us have sinned, but there is no real connection between the sin of Adam and the sin of mankind, other than it could be said that Adam's sin is typical of the rest of us.

A second view has been called the *"legal interpretation."* This holds that Adam was the representative of mankind and that the human race shares in the deed of its representative. But a representative must be chosen by the people he represents. None of us participated in choosing Adam.

The third view is that what we *"inherit"* from Adam is the tendency to sin. This is true. But this is not what Paul was saying. It would not suit his argument at all.

William Barclay goes on to simply restate what Paul has already stated, which is the only possible interpretation of this passage. Barclay calls it the *realistic interpretation*. This interpretation says that all mankind, literally and actually, sinned in Adam. Paradise was lost in the Garden of Eden at the very moment that Adam disobeyed.

Yet each of us is his own Adam. We too have disobeyed. In some way Adam is an unelected representative of us in that he functioned as we function. In some way we inherit from Adam our tendency to sin. But these are only quaint views of sin. The real issue is that all of us have sinned and come short of the glory of God because of Adam. Read Paul's exact words:

> Therefore as sin came into the world through one man and death through sin, and so death spread to all men because all men sinned — sin indeed was in the world before the

law was given, but sin is not counted where there is no law. Yet death reigned from Adam to Moses, even over those whose sins were not like the transgression of Adam, who was a type of the one who was to come (Romans 5:12-14).

In Adam all the children of Adam actually partook of his nature. Just as he turned to sin, we too all turn to sin. Paul notes that there was a major gap of time between the fall of Adam and the time that Moses introduced the Ten Commandments and the rest of the law. Still, what was right was right, and what was wrong was wrong, even if mankind did not have the Commandments.

To illustrate, a man bought a large plot of land but did not fence it in. Five years afterward he put a fence around it. Putting up the fence did not make it his land. It was his land all the time. But putting up the fence showed the limits of his property. So it is with the law. It puts up a fence to indicate where the boundary line actually is. As Paul says, "But sin is not counted where there is no law" (Romans 5:13). He is saying that you would not condemn anyone for driving into the other man's field if there was no fence to warn him. Then he goes on to say sin reigned from Adam to Moses, even if the individual people, the children of Adam, didn't do the same wrong that Adam did.

III

Paul is endeavoring to underline two basic facts of life.

First, there is a solidarity to the human race. We are all in precisely the same predicament. I am a sinner. You are a sinner. You and I were born that way because of Adam.

So the crisis is universal. All humanity is seen in equal terms. What Paul is teaching is referred to theologically as the doctrine of original sin. What may come as a surprise to you is that for Paul the doctrine of original sin is a doctrine in behalf of man, not against him.

Earl Palmer, in his commentary on Romans entitled

Salvation by Surprise, notes that this concept of solidarity of all persons sweeps away every pretense of the superiority of one person over/against another. He describes the doctrine. It is like several ship passengers who happen to get washed overboard in the mid-Atlantic. The reasons for slipping off the deck vary from individual to individual. Each one retains his distinctiveness in the water as on the deck. But as each one discovers his own plight and finds his companions are also in the same cold water, it is meaningless to discuss or debate degrees of fault. They are all in the water. It doesn't make any difference whether one was traveling first-class or economy, whether one was a good Jew or a pagan. It doesn't make any difference whether one had great swimming skill and the others didn't. The need of each of these persons thrashing around in the water is a total need.

Second, this passage explains the original cause of death and the present reality of death that we all face.

The sin of Adam initiated both physical and spiritual death. Death was not God's intention. He had warned Adam, "You may freely eat of every tree of the garden; but of the tree of knowledge of good and evil you shall not eat, for in the day that you eat of it you shall die" (Genesis 2:16-17).

Physical death did not come immediately. Spiritual death came first. Because of their disobedience, Adam and Eve began to view each other differently. No longer was their nakedness uncomplicated and natural. They began to distance themselves from each other. They covered themselves. They couldn't handle intimacy in the way they had handled it before. Spiritual death dehumanizes. We need to look only into our own fractured lives to see how rampant the dehumanizing process is. We see the brokenness that is the result of sin. Alienation and separation are the hallmarks of our human condition.

The natural outflow of this is physical death. It is a

present reality for all of us. We don't want to talk about it or think about it. Yet every one of us is simply one breath away from death. So a 49-year-old actor, David Jannsen, can pass a physical, appear to be in the best of health and die in his sleep. One fact of life for every single one of us is death unless Jesus Christ returns before that day.

The cause of death, spiritual and physical, is the fall of Adam. That is the biblical truth Paul drives home in this passage. We see our solidarity in this.

IV

Having established that there was a literal Adam, having articulated that the existence of sin in the human race comes directly from Adam, and having sketched our solidarity as human beings and the fact of our spiritual and physical death, Paul sketches some contrasts.

The greatest contrast of all is that we are not limited to one Adam. There is a second Adam. Paradise lost is now Paradise found. Ours is a total need that needs some total help. Not only is there guilt, there is grace. And it all finds its summary in the fact that there is a second Adam.

Paul explodes into his verbal contrast between the first Adam, the Adam of Genesis, and the second Adam, the Adam named Jesus Christ. Read his words that say it so much better than can anyone else:

> But the free gift is not like the trespass. For if many died through one man's trespass, much more have the grace of God and the free gift in the grace of that one man Jesus Christ abounded for many. And the free gift is not like the effect of that one man's sin. For the judgment following one trespass brought condemnation, but the free gift following many trespasses brings justification. If, because of one man's trespass, death reigned through that one man, much more will those who receive the abundance of grace and the free gift of righteousness reign in life through the

one man Jesus Christ. Then as one man's trespass led to condemnation for all men, so one man's act of righteousness leads to acquittal and life for all men. For as by one man's disobedience many were made sinners, so by one man's obedience many will be made righteous. Law came in, to increase the trespass; but where sin increased, grace abounded all the more, so that as sin reigned in death, grace also may reign through righteousness to eternal life through Jesus Christ our Lord (Romans 5:15-21).

Paul is saying that we are helpless, that we are overwhelmed. Most of us believe we are so self-secure that just the thought of being helpless does not really register. But whether we choose to acknowledge it or not is not the issue. The One who knows us best has told us that it's true.

We've all experienced helplessness of one kind or another. Back in the late 1950s our family had a lovely lakeside home in Indiana, where my father was president of a summer theological seminary. There was a little creek that wound through our property behind our house and emptied into the lake.

For a brief period of time one summer my sister and I lived in that home by ourselves while my parents were out of the country. During their absence torrential rains swept across northern Indiana, and our innocent little creek became a swollen river. My sister and I tried to reinforce the creek bank, but it didn't work. The creek broadened its path and began its advance toward the house. At first it crawled around the house and on into the lake. It soon made its way into the floor vents. As the water crawled toward the doorways we hooked up pumps. We tried to sweep the water away but our best efforts were to no avail — the house began to flood. First an inch, then two, then three. The wall-to-wall carpeting began to float. When the waters finally receded we had a sodden mess of ruined carpet, warped cabinets, mud deposits, and a sickish looking water line on all the walls about eighteen inches from the floor. To this day I can still remember the frustration of trying to actually push the water away.

What was needed was a whole new beginning for that house. At first we hoped the problem would go away. But twice more in the next several years the floods rushed through our house. A cleanup crew scooped out the mud and threw away everything that could not be salvaged. Painters came in and redecorated. What carpet could be cleaned, stretched, and relaid was put back into place, with fresh padding. There had to be a total refurbishing. Ultimately the whole house had to be raised high above the level of any possible future flooding. And the creek flow had to be regulated by the government flood control.

That is precisely what Jesus came to do. He came to refurbish, recreate, and restore. He came to conquer death. He came to eliminate guilt. He came to give a new beginning. He came to offer you His unmerited favor. What a contrast with the mess made by the first Adam. Jesus's cleanup is a free gift. You don't have to buy it. But you do have to confront the reality of your need and receive it.

We can all look real religious and see ourselves as good people, never having confronted the desperate condition that is ours. Sin is sin. It is ghastly. It brings death. And God wants you to have life. Every one of us, no matter how sophisticated or how simple, no matter how discouraged and messed up or how fairly well put together, must be gripped anew with the reality of what God has done for us in Jesus Christ. It may mean praying the prayer of repentance, inviting the new Adam into your life on the basis of His death and resurrection. For others it may mean stopping, contemplating, rejoicing, and celebrating the amazing grace that we have received and dare never take for granted.

Now What Is Our Response to Be? 10

Now what is our response to be? Shall we sin to our heart's content and see how far we can exploit the grace of God? What a ghastly thought! We, who have died to sin — how could we live in sin a moment longer? (Romans 6:1-2, J.B. Phillips).

THE APOSTLE PAUL has now declared two great doctrinal truths.

First, he has sketched our human condition for us. The picture he presents isn't very pleasant. He's devoted most of the first three chapters of Romans to describing our sinful nature and our rebellion against God. Every one of us, no matter how religious, has not met the standard of God's righteousness. We are condemned with spiritual and physical death. The first Adam disobeyed God. All of us are implicated in that first man's act of the will. For some of us, our rebellion is active. We wave our fist in God's face. For others of us, it is passive. We shuffle along independent of him. That's the bad news.

Paul then moved into a transition in Romans 3:21, taking the next two-and-a-half chapters to tell us about the good news. He describes what God has done for us in Jesus Christ, the second Adam. He lets us know that there's nothing you and I can do to earn a right relationship with God. We are only made right with God through Christ. He has paid the penalty of our sin, and offers you and me forgiveness. There is no longer any condemnation to those who are in Christ. "Jesus paid it all/All to Him I owe/Sin had left its crimson stain/He washed it white as snow." The freedom is purchased.

But you say, "He couldn't forgive me the things I've done. I carry around some guilt that could never be taken away. I don't like to talk about it, but I've done some things that have pretty well destroyed some other people and just about destroyed me. I don't qualify for any gift. All I've earned is condemnation." Paul says that that is a lie. He states, "Where sin increased, grace abounded all the more so that, as sin reigned in death, grace also might reign through righteousness to eternal life through Jesus Christ our Lord" (Romans 5:20-21). God is telling you that there is nothing you've done that cannot be forgiven.

Romans 5:20-21 delivered the crushing blow to legalistic religion. You can't buy God's favor. Your good works are not the means to salvation. Actually, they can make you proud, self-centered, and self-righteous. However, even as Paul has declared the fact that you can't buy the favor of God with your good works, he also warns that it's a terrible thing to "rip off" the mercy of God.

That's how he starts off chapter six. He knows that there are some people who are only interested in getting hold of a one-way ticket to heaven. They have a sneaking suspicion that somehow they'll be accountable at some future day of judgment for how they've lived their lives in this world. The Gospel is good news to them because they know that they'll never be able to stand in the day of judgment on the basis of their works. So the idea of salvation being a free gift sounds very very good. This person is out to grab anything free he can get. He takes that one-way ticket to heaven, holds it tight in his grubby little fist, and proceeds to live like hell here on earth.

Paul is very aware that some people respond this way. So he opens chapter six with this terse question:

> Now what is our response to be? Shall we sin to our heart's content and see how far we can exploit the grace of God? What a ghastly thought! We, who have died to sin — how

could we live in sin a moment longer? (Romans 6:1-2, J. B. Phillips).

The Holy Spirit had given Paul the wisdom to realize that on one hand some people would lock themselves into a bondage of salvation by works. They would go to church faithfully. They would serve on the boards. They would totally exhaust themselves trying to win the favor of God. That kind of legalism receives a devastating blow in the first five chapters of Romans. Now, the Holy Spirit helps Paul swing around to speak to the other extreme. There are cynical exploiters who cry out, "Whoopee! More sin, more grace, more sin, more grace. Hey, this is all right." Those who work so hard to earn their salvation are caught up in the heresy of legalism. Those who hold on so tightly to that one-way ticket to heaven, then do whatever they want to do, are caught up in the heresy of antinomianism. This is the notion that since we are justified by God's free grace and not at all by our merit, there is no reason for us to live an ethical and moral life.

You and I know that there are several ways to raise children. One is to do it by fear. It works for a while. You scare your children into being obedient. You threaten them with harsh spankings. You refuse to take any back talk from them by meeting their timid effort at it with a slap in the face. If they displease you, you withdraw your affection, manipulating them by the loneliness of rejection. Sooner or later they'll come to despair. The only way they'll be able to survive with some kind of psychic health is to reject you. They can't survive the emotional manipulation you're dishing out. They need love and acceptance. They need your care. If they are ruled by fear, they'll have to go underground with their emotions. They'll not have that sense of freedom to go through the developmental stages of childhood, adolescence, and young adulthood. Their self-esteem may be crushed. They may need extensive therapy to really believe they're worth anything. The parent who orchestrates his children by fear probably will have to pay an awesome price when they wise up and realize what's happened to them.

There's an alternative model. It's the one of the loving, caring, reasoning parent. This parent is willing to serve the children. The parent believes in eyeball-to-eyeball conversation. He's sensitive to the developmental stages through which most children go. More important, however, is that he's honest about his own failures. He tells his children the difference between right and wrong. He opens the Bible and tells them what God has revealed about how to live life the smart way, the intelligent way, the wise way. He's not flustered when they disagree. He knows that they have to think through the issues. He can't force his standards and his beliefs on them. They have a right to reject them or to at least put them in suspended animation. This way, when they ultimately endorse these biblical ideals, they have endorsed them as their own. It is not just a hand-me-down-faith or an inherited set of rules.

There's something exciting about watching a wise parent communicate his own weakness, his own vulnerability. There's something refreshing about hearing him say to his child, "I want you to know that as strong as I believe what I've told you, there's nothing that you can ever do that will make me turn you out. You are always my child. There is nothing you could ever do to cause me to turn my back on you."

You sort of understand it when the first child rebels against the manipulative, unreasoning, harsh, arbitrary parent. But there's hardly anything more offensive in the world than to see an insensitive teenager or young adult slap a caring, loving, open, reasonable parent in the face as he tries to take advantage of his freedom. He demeans the very person who has made available the kindly discipline undergirded by unconditional love.

You and I are part of God's family if we've received the free gift. You and I are set free of the fear of punishment. We have the privilege of confessing our sins. But we have no right to "rip off" the mercy of God. You and I have been born anew by the Spirit of God. We have been through a cleansing process with Jesus Christ.

II

Paul describes this process of cleansing in graphic terms understood by the New Testament believers. It's the terminology of baptism.

The Christians to whom Paul wrote understood clearly that baptism has to it a symbolic significance. As one went down into the water, he was identifying with the death of Jesus Christ. When he was under the water, he was identifying with the burial of Jesus Christ. When he came up out of the water, he was identifying with the resurrection of Jesus Christ. That's why Paul declares so emphatically:

> What shall we say then? Are we to continue in sin that grace may abound? By no means! How can we who died to sin still live in it? Do you not know that all of us who have been baptized into Christ Jesus were baptized into his death? We were buried therefore with him by baptism into his death, so that as Christ was raised from the dead by the glory of the Father, we too might walk in newness of life (Romans 6:1-4).

Then Paul goes on to make the analogy with the death of Christ more forceful:

> For if we have been united with him in a death like his, we shall certainly be united with him in a resurrection like his. We know that our old self was crucified with him so that the sinful body might be destroyed, and we might no longer be enslaved to sin. For he who has died is freed from sin. But if we have died with Christ, we believe that we shall also live with him. For we know that Christ being raised from the dead will never die again; death no longer

has dominion over him. The death he died he died to sin, once for all, but the life he lives he lives to God. So you also must consider yourselves dead to sin and alive to God in Christ Jesus (Romans 6:5-11).

What Paul is trying to get across to you and me is that the old has passed away. The new is here. Whereas the first Adam led you and me into death, the second Adam, Jesus Christ, has led you and me into life. Whereas the natural extension of the law is into legalism, we now live under grace. We no longer are marked by unrighteousness. We now stand in a position of righteousness before God.

But some of us who pride ourselves in grace still have a legalistic approach to the Christian faith. We hold to "cheap grace." Paul is really saying, "Why do you, who are dead to sin and alive in Christ, choose to keep the stinking, rotting remains of the old corpse in the living room?"

I once heard a preacher tell a story he heard from a seminary professor. Perhaps it's aprocryphal. It's about a lady who lived in Alabama. Her beloved husband died. Instead of having him placed in a casket and buried in the ground, she had him embalmed, seated on a chair, and placed inside an airtight glass case she had placed in her living room. Everyday when she left the house she would say goodbye to him. When she came home she'd say hello. She carried on her imaginary conversations with his ever-present corpse. Sometime later, she went on a world trip. While traveling through Europe, she met a wonderful man. He proposed to her, and she accepted. She brought him home to her Alabama town. Imagine his amazement when she ushered him into her living room. He exclaimed, "Who's that sitting there?" She replied, "That's my husband." It wasn't long before the corpse of the former husband found a different resting place. The new husband, as loving and kind as he may have been, would not tolerate her morbid fascination with the past. Nor does God take much joy in the ways in which we continue to relive our old life. He wants to get rid of the corpse. Ours is a new relationship. Ours is a living friendship.

III

Paul uses three particular words to remind us of the new position we have in Christ whenever we get to flirting with the old life, when Satan would try to seduce us once again into a life that's lived like hell while we make insipid claims of God's grace. Paul urges us to keep these three words in our mind.

The first is the word *know*. In Romans 6:3, he reminds us that we *know* that those of us who have been baptized into Christ were baptized into His death. In verse six, he alerts us to the fact that we *know* that our old self was crucified with Christ so that the sinful body might be destroyed and we might no longer be enslaved to sin. In verse nine he points out that we *know* that Christ, being raised from the dead, will never die again, and, therefore, death need have no dominion over us, even as it has no dominion over Him.

Then he introduces a second word. This word is *consider*. In verses eleven and twelve he writes, "So you also must consider yourselves dead to sin and alive to God in Christ Jesus. Let not sin therefore reign in your mortal bodies, to make you obey their passions." He's urging you to understand your position before God, which is that you are dead to sin and alive to God in Christ Jesus. There's no need for sin to reign. You are no longer its slave.

Then he comes up with a third word. The word is *yield*. In verses thirteen and fourteen he writes, "Do not yield your members to sin as instruments of wickedness, but yield yourselves to God as men who have been brought from death to life, and your members to God as instruments of righteousness. For sin will have no dominion over you, since you are not under law but under grace." You and I have the privilege of choosing whether or not to be instruments of wickedness or of righteousness. You and I are called to yield ourselves: to be voluntarily those who are God's instruments; to yearn to live lives of victory; to live lives that are righteous.

God calls you to put yourself in His hands. The new birth you have experienced if you have repented of sin and put your trust in Jesus Christ is more than a belief in dogmas. Faith does involve cognitive data. But more than that, it involves a personal relationship with the living God. You are privileged to enter into daily fellowship with Him. Yours is one of trust in a caring, loving, personal God. Yours is one of potential obedience to Him, really believing that His word is designed for your good, for your welfare. When He says don't do something, it isn't to spoil your fun. It's to enhance the quality of your life. You are privileged to live in a love relationship with the God of the universe. That's what the Christian faith is all about.

Some of us love to skate on thin ice. We get our kicks out of living a daring existence.

It reminds me of my youthful years in Boston. There was a pond about a mile from my house. It was called Spy Pond. It was quite deep. Toward the end of November or early December, it would begin to freeze. We would take our hockey gear and go down and mark off an area that was well frozen and play our games. However, as is the natural inclination of youngsters, we would get a little bit daring. We would move off of the area the township had declared as safe ice and skate out toward the middle of the pond. We could see that the ice was getting thinner and thinner. But there was something in each of us that wanted to see how close we could get to the water rippling over the edge of the thin ice without cracking the surface and falling in. So we skated out. We'd get closer and closer. We'd begin to feel the movement of the ice underneath us. And we'd hear those strange moaning, groaning sounds. Most of us would quickly skate back to the thick ice. Inevitably, someone would go too far and crash into the cold, cold water. In some cases, the fire department would have to bring a hook and ladder and stretch it over the ice to offer a retreat for the safety of any pathetic soul whose daring proved foolish.

A life committed to Christ is not one that sees how close it can get to returning to its former existence. It is one that really desires to be conformed to the image of God. Are you skating on thin ice? Are you trying to see how close you can come to life as it is lived in the flesh and get by with it instead of living life in the Spirit of Jesus Christ?

IV

Charles R. Swindoll, pastor of the Evangelical Free Church in Fullerton, California, describes two radically different approaches to the Christian life in light of the sixth chapter of Romans. He says you can choose between a "corrective" and a "preventive" theology. You can decide that you're going to see what you can get by with in life and when you fail run quickly to Jesus and ask him for forgiveness. Or, you can actually find the equipment of the Holy Spirit to live a life that is oriented toward righteousness.

He illustrates it in relationship to his own experience in teaching his son how to drive. He says that there are two ways he could have taught. One is the corrective way. He could have given him a lesson in first aid. He could have shown him where all the hospitals are on a map of Orange County. He could have given him insurance forms with extensive instruction as to how to fill them out and how to quickly process a claim. That would be the corrective way. The assumption is that there is going to be an accident and you had better get yourself ready for it.

The other approach is the preventive way of teaching one's son to drive. This is simply instructing him how to drive safely. It's a positive approach. The whole presupposition is that driving is good. By learning some basic rules you can drive year after year without an accident. Granted, accidents can happen. It's good to be aware of what to do in those situations. But it's better to think positively, applying oneself to safety.

Many of us have cut our teeth on corrective theology. We are always talking about confession and what we do now since we have fallen again into sin. You and I are privileged to claim 1 John 1:9: "If we confess our sins, he is faithful and just, and will forgive our sins and cleanse us from all unrighteousness." Better still, we have the privilege of living, in John, chapter fifteen, as branches that are grafted into the very Vine itself, Jesus Christ, deriving a positive life flow that comes from constant living relationship with Him.

You have a power available to you through the Holy Spirit that can enable you to live a life of victory. Yours is not that little ticket to heaven, that fire escape from hell. Yours is eternal life in this life. Claim Christ's promise of release and learn to live in the freedom He purchased with His blood.

Who's in Charge Here? 11

*When you were slaves of sin, you were free in regard
to righteousness. But then what return did you get
from the things of which you are now ashamed? The
end of those things is death. But now that you have
been set free from sin and have become slaves of God,
the return you get is sanctification and its end,
eternal life (Romans 6:20-22).*

ARE YOU AWARE that you may be a slave? No,
slavery wasn't eliminated by the Emancipation Proc-
lamation. Not only may you be a slave, but you may be
working and living with people who are slaves.

Some of us are slaves to our jobs. We're workaholics.
We are driven to perform. Some males find the greatest
part of our identity in what we do. One of the first questions we ask when we meet a new person is, "What is your
work?" Seldom do we ask, "What kind of a person are
you?"

Some of us are slaves to laziness. It's difficult for us to
get motivated. We have various kinds of rationalizations.
One thing for sure, we just don't like to work. We're slaves
to indolence.

Some of us are slaves to things. We have let our possessions dominate our lives and are seldom satisfied with
what we have. We want more. We're involved in the
endless pursuit of things. We find ourselves enormously
frustrated when those things begin to break, and we discover that they are costly to repair.

Some of us are slaves to other people. We spend our
time trying to please an employer, our colleagues, our
partner, our children, our parents, our friends. We are
easily orchestrated. People can manipulate us by guilt.

The raised eyebrow sends daggers through us. Much of modern psychology is devoted to uncovering our subconscious desires for acceptance.

Some of us are slaves to ourselves. We have self-destructive habits. We have political viewpoints that control us. We have prejudices that hold us in captivity. We have resentments that will not let go. We are in self-bondage.

The apostle Paul has some very terse things to say about slavery. He tells us that in an ultimate sense you and I have the option of choosing between two kinds of slavery. You and I have the God-given privilege of choosing between being slaves of sin or slaves of righteousness.

Paul was writing to Roman believers who lived in a slave culture. It is difficult for us to identify with that kind of slavery. We know what it is to be slaves to a job, things, people, and habits. We don't fully understand what it is to be owned by another person. It's not part of our experience. We work for other people. We have employers who purchase eight hours from us each day. During those hours in which we are literally or figuratively "punched-in," we know that we are responsible to work for them. To some extent we are servants. However, we know that according to the law of our country those employers have no right to assume that they own us. There are limits to the number of hours they can make us work. If they try to exploit us we have the privilege of finding another employer who's more considerate. Our employer pays us for what we do during the time that we are at his disposal. When that time ends we're free to do exactly as we choose.

In Paul's time the status of the slave was quite different. At no time did he belong to himself. He had no moment when he was free. He was the exclusive possession of his master.

Paul picks up that picture, alerting believers in Jesus

Christ to the fact that, whereas we were once slaves of sin, we are now under new ownership. Whereas once we were in bondage to Satan, now we are owned by Christ. As Jesus said in his Sermon on the Mount, "No one can serve two masters; for either he will hate the one and love the other, or he will be devoted to the one and despise the other. You cannot serve God and mammon" (Matthew 6:24).

Paul is trying to tell us that you and I have to decide who's in charge. We have already looked at the heresy of antinomianism. We saw how some believers have cheapened God's grace, using His unconditional grace, His unconditional love, His unconditional favor, to go and slap Him in the face. Paul continues to write on this theme:

> What then? Are we to sin because we are not under law but under grace? By no means! Do you not know that if you yield yourselves to any one as obedient slaves, you are slaves of the one whom you obey, either of sin, which leads to death, or of obedience, which leads to righteousness? But thanks be to God, that you who were once slaves of sin have become obedient from the heart to the standard of teaching to which you were committed, and, having been set free from sin, have become slaves of righteousness. I am speaking in human terms, because of your natural limitations. For just as you once yielded your members to impurity and to greater and greater iniquity, so now yield your members to righteousness for sanctification (Romans 6:15-19).

Our original slavery was to sin. This was an involuntary slavery. There was nothing you and I could do about it. Sin is a cruel slave master that repays those who are under its power with death.

Paul paints a contrast. Those of us who have repented of sin and put our trust in Jesus Christ have died with Christ, and have been reborn with Him. We have a new set of options before us. Whereas in our former state we were involuntarily oriented toward sin, we now have the voluntary option of choosing our master.

Some of us who have been set free from the condemnation of sin are orienting ourselves back toward our former lifestyles. We're trying to figure out how close we can come to how we lived before without getting caught. We are volunteering for bondage.

Where on the other hand we have appropriated a new lifestyle, we are aware now that we are slaves of Christ. We are orienting our lives to righteousness.

Take a look at the contrasting costs and payoffs. Stop to contemplate what it is to be under the ownership of sin or under the ownership of Christ.

It's possible to be enslaved and to think that you are free. That's the life of the nonbeliever. The costs of this existence are minimal. The nonbeliever has no responsibility toward righteousness. It's an easy life. He floats downstream with the current. He does what he wants to do. He's taken slave. However, the payoffs are not very pleasant — death, alienation, bondage and guilt. One who has not repented of sin and put his trust in Jesus Christ is spiraling downward. Paul refers to it as yielding "your members to impurity and to greater and greater iniquity."

It's also possible to be Christ's own, to be one who chooses to become Christ's slave. You and I can be persons under new ownership. The costs are much greater. We have a higher standard of living. We are forced to say no to our old nature. Ours is not a life of rationalizations to see how close we can get to our former existence. It is one of discipline. It is one of strength. The payoffs are enormous. For ours is a life of potential victory in Christ. We are persons who are not spiraling downward but are spiraling upward. We have yielded our "members to righteousness for sanctification." Our position is one of being righteous before God. That doesn't mean that everything we do is right. It means that we are accepted by Him on the basis of what He has done for us, and now His Holy Spirit is leading us forward. We no longer have to handle our life in our own strength. We are empowered by Him.

The exciting aspect of being under His new ownership is that we are given an energy source. It's a supply that is never depleted. You and I have union with Jesus Christ.

Some of us view the Christian life as if we are on one side of a large lake. On the other side is heaven. We're responsible to swim across that lake. That isn't what the Scriptures tell us. God has given us a boat with a motor on it, and He has provided all of the energy that motor needs to propel us across that lake to the other side. When you and I come to Christ it's as if we're at the lobby level of an eighty-story building. Some of us are insistent on trying to climb to the eightieth floor by way of the stairs when God has placed an elevator in the building that will take us to the top floor. You don't have to walk to New York. You're privileged to fly. God's providing the vehicle and energy source. Whereas the nonbeliever floats downstream with the current, we are empowered to move upstream against the contemporary flow of life.

It's important to count the contrasting costs and the payoffs between the life of the believer and the nonbeliever.

Five years ago, twenty-five Protestant clergymen were invited to spend fifteen days at the Vatican in Rome. Each morning we entered into intensive conversations with one of the cardinals and his colleagues at the secretariat over which he presided. It was a fascinating ecumenical exchanging of ideas. On several of the afternoons we were entertained by the heads of the various holy orders. One of the most fascinating experiences was to spend an entire day with the head of the Benedictine Order. We traveled with him to Subiaco, a village forty miles from Rome. It was there, in a hillside cave, that St. Benedict took up his abode, spending three years of his opening manhood in solitary prayer, contemplation, and austerity. Out of his personal discipline came the Benedictine Order.

I'm told that when a man wishes to become a member of the great Benedictine Order of monks, he's accepted for a year on probation. During all that time the clothes that he wore in the world hang in his cell. At any time he can take off his monk's habit, put on his worldly clothes, and walk out. No one will think any the worse of him. Only at the end of the year are his clothes finally taken away. By that time he must know what he is doing. He must enter the order with open eyes and a full appreciation of the commitment he is making.

Likewise, Jesus wants you to count the cost of being His disciple. Coming to Him isn't just the result of one emotional moment in your life. There is a cost. There is a distinction between the old life and the new life. Jesus wants you to count the cost and make the decision about who's in charge.

Not only is there a distinction between a nonbeliever and a believer. Not only is it possible to be enslaved and think you're free, and possible to be free and live like you're free. There is a third alternative. It is possible to be free and live like you are enslaved. That's the most miserable type of life a person can live. It's the life of what the Bible calls the carnal Christian (1 Corinthians 3:1-4). The carnal Christian is a person who never allows the old clothes to be taken away. He has accepted Christ. He's joined the order. But periodically, he slips into his old clothes and goes out on the town. He's a person who is, in the words of the prophet Elijah, "limping between two opinions." He's trying to play the middle of the road. He wears the label Christian, but he's trying to serve two masters.

Paul describes this person with one of the strongest analogies you'll ever find in the Scriptures. He refers to him as being a spiritual bigamist. He does this in the early verses of chapter seven when he notes that a married woman is bound by the law to her husband as long as he lives. If her husband dies, she is freed from her marriage vows and is entitled to remarry. However, if she lives with another man while her husband is still alive, she's an adulteress. Paul is telling you and me that we died to the old slave-master: sin, the law. And now we belong to Jesus Christ. We are the recipients of free gift that is eternal life. Ours is no longer an involuntary slavery to sin, nor is it a voluntary slavery to sin. But some of us are trying to serve two masters. We are spiritual adulterers. We are carrying on a conscious, deliberate, voluntary love affair with sin while claiming to be Christ's.

Paul says you and I don't have to live that way. We've gotten rid of the involuntary bondage. Why voluntarily submit ourselves to it once again? Why live under the old written code when we are privileged to live "in the new life of the spirit" (Romans 7:6).

Paul is describing the Christian life the way it was designed to be lived. He has shown the contrast between the condemnation of the law and the freedom of grace. He is urging you and me to decide once and for all whose slave we will be. It's a decision fleshed out in struggle and pain. Paul is clear. The realities of spiritual living dare not be papered over.

Who's in charge here? Who do you want to serve? Who owns you? Are you still in captivity to Satan? Or are you Christ's? And if you are Christ's, do you want to live a life of defeat or do you yearn for a life of victory? One thing is for certain, you dare not "rip off" God's grace, trying to claim all the blessings He promises while refusing to allow Him the place of recognized lordship.

The Inner Struggle 12

*For I do not do the good I want, but the evil I do not
want is what I do. Now if I do what I do not want, it is
no longer I that do it, but sin which dwells within me
(Romans 7:19-20).*

THUS FAR Paul has confronted us with the doctrine of sin. He has moved on to describe justification
by faith. Now he is developing the doctrine of sanctification.

Just as physical and emotional life has its developmental stages, so does spiritual life. The apostle Peter talks
about newborn babies needing milk. In the same way,
those of us who are recently born anew by the Spirit of
God need spiritual milk. Then we move past that bland,
liquid diet to a more substantial food intake. The believer
in Christ is in a constant maturation process, with all of its
potential for positive, steady growth or some unfortunate
disruptions that can label you and me as cases of arrested
development.

Right now, in the middle of this section dealing with the
doctrine of sanctification, Paul stops to make a fascinating
description of our human situation.

I

He begins by sharing some perceptive insights about
the Old Testament law. He points out that although you
and I are now in Christ, set free from the bondage of the
law, this does not mean that the law is bad. We live in a
society that puts a premium on "newness." That which is

old is fit only for the junk pile, unless perchance it is so old that it becomes quaint.

We live with planned obsolescence. What is new is good. What is old is bad. So whether it be a rock group, poster girl, clothing fashion, or an automobile style, the new is considered to be correct.

This simply isn't the case with the Old and New Testament. Jesus did not come to abolish the Old Covenant. He came to fulfill it. He did not come to say that the law was bad. He came to enable you and me to live free from the captivity to salvation by works. It so subtly becomes our orientation when we confront the legal standards of the law. The Old and New Testaments are not two different religions. They are the same religion. The God of the Old Testament is also the God of the New Testament. The God of the Old Testament is not simply a God of wrath. He's the God of love who at the very moment of Adam and Eve's rebellion promises that One will come who will crush the head of the serpent. He provides a ram on Mount Moriah to serve as a substitute for the sacrifice of Isaac. He's the God who hears the cry of His alienated people chafing under the yoke of slavery in Egypt. He offers them the Paschal Lamb, saying, "When I see the blood I will pass over you." He leads them out of Egypt. Their annual commemoration of that event continues to kindle the hope that the promised One will come. The prophet Isaiah and others describe the Lamb of God which taketh away the sin of the world.

On that Holy Thursday evening in the upper room, as Jesus pauses to celebrate the Passover with His disciples, the Old Covenant is not abolished — it is fulfilled. He breaks the bread, saying, "This is my body broken for you." He takes the cup, saying, "This is my blood shed for the remission of sin." Then the next day He's crucified and buried. On the third He rises from the dead. The bondage of sin is abolished. We enter into the era of the new covenant — a fulfillment of the promises of God through all of human history. In fact, the work of atonement has implications not only for the present and future. The only way to right relationship with the father is through Jesus Christ. It is faith in God's provision that makes the difference. So although our bondage to the law is over, it is still important that we become aware of the three primary ways in which the law functions.

First, the law defines sin. "What then shall we say? That the law is sin? By no means! Yet, if it had not been for the law, I should not have known sin" (Romans 7:7a).

The law enables you and me to know the clear distinctions between right and wrong. Paul has already told us that built in the human conscience there is a moral sensitivity. However, that basic instinct is educated by the law. Whether or not we know the law, we still do some things that are right and some that are wrong. It's only as we know the ground rules that we can clearly distinguish between the two.

Every so often our family gets involved in a big free-for-all fight. It comes while we're playing Monopoly. We all have a basic feel for the game. The fight is usually over some specific problem as to how we're going to play the game. How many throws of the dice are there to be before you can get out of jail? Can you borrow money from another player without mortgaging your properties? They are silly little debates that can take a lot of time if you don't have a rule book. The best way to settle the argument quickly is to read the rules. The best way to keep the argument going is to have floating rules because you don't take the time to consult the rule book.

The law defines sin. Without it, all of our clever rationalizations would make more sense. I can give you plenty of good reasons why a certain street should have a two-way traffic flow. However, if there's a one-way sign on it and I choose to go the opposite way, I have not only endangered my life, I have broken the law.

Second, the law actually provokes sin. "I should not have known what it is to covet if the law had not said, 'You shall not covet.' But sin, finding opportunity in the commandment, wrought in me all kinds of covetousness" (Romans 7:7b-8a).

Tell me not to covet, so what do I do? I start wanting to covet.

I'm not interested in seeing some exploitive movie such as "10" until I discover it's something I shouldn't see if I want to keep my thoughts clean. Then I am curious, and I want what I know isn't good for me. I may even make a rationalization that any self-respecting pastor who wants to be in touch with what some of the people he ministers to are seeing should see it.

Put up a "no entrance" sign, and I am suddenly interested in entering what never really interested me before.

That's what happened to poor old Adam and Eve in the garden. God said don't eat, and they compulsively couldn't think of much else. Just imagine all the other fine trees that were around. Think of all the other delicious fruit. None of it looked so good as the fruit that was forbidden. Saint Augustine, in his *Confessions* describes his own fascination with the forbidden thing:

> There was a pear tree near our vineyard, laden with fruit. One stormy night we rascally youths set out to rob it and carry our spoils away. We took off a huge load of pears...not to feast upon ourselves, but to throw them to the pigs, though we ate just enough to have the pleasure of forbidden fruit. They were nice pears, but it was not the pears that my wretched soul coveted, for I had plenty better at home. I picked them simply in order to become a thief. The only feast I got was a feast of iniquity, and that I

enjoyed to the full. What was it that I loved in that theft? Was it the pleasure of acting against the law, in order that I, a prisoner under rules, might have a maimed counterfeit of freedom by doing what was forbidden, with a dim similitude of impotence?...The desire to steal was awakened simply by the prohibition of stealing.

Third, the law exposes the very cancer of sin itself: "Did that which is good, then, bring death to me? By no means! It was sin, working death in me through what is good, in order that sin might be shown to be sin, and through the commandment might become sinful beyond measure" (Romans 7:13).

II

Now Paul comes to one of the most significant parts of his letter to the church at Rome. He describes the tension and inner struggle that is ours:

We know that the law is spiritual; but I am carnal, sold under sin. I do not understand my own actions. For I do not do what I want, but I do the very thing I hate. Now if I do what I do not want, I agree that the law is good. So then it is no longer I that do it, but sin which dwells within me. For I know that nothing good dwells within me, that is, in my flesh. I can will what is right, but I cannot do it. For I do not do the good I want, but the evil I do not want is what I do. Now if I do what I do not want, it is no longer I that do it, but sin which dwells within me.

So I find it to be a law that when I want to do right, evil lies close at hand. For I delight in the law of God, in my inmost self, but I see in my members another law at war with the law of my mind and making me captive to the law of sin which dwells in my members. Wretched man that I am! Who will deliver me from this body of death? Thanks be to God through Jesus Christ our Lord! So then, I of myself serve the law of God with my mind, but with my flesh I serve the law of sin (Romans 7:14-25).

Bible scholars through the centuries have argued over what is the actual intent of Paul's words. When he talks about an inner warfare, is he speaking of his former days in his life before he trusted Jesus Christ for salvation? Or is he sharing out of his Christian journey following salvation but prior to sanctification, that subsequent fullness of the Holy Spirit? Or is Paul telling of his struggle as a Christian in the very midst of the sanctification process?

There are those who hold to option one. They say that Paul's argument is subjective. They believe that this struggle describes the status of a person who is under the law and that it is being described by one who is now freed from the bondage of sin.

There are those who hold to option two. They take the position that Paul was describing a person who put his trust in Jesus Christ but had not yet discovered the secret of life lived in the fullness of the Holy Spirit. He had not come to grips with the possibility of the victorious Christian life.

I believe that these first two options have some validity to them. The person without Christ is a person driven by inner impulses that almost defy his explanation. He knows there's a good and an evil. Part of him is driven by a satanic motivation. Part of him wants to be a good person. I will go so far as to say that a person who is a believer in Jesus Christ, who has not discovered some of the exciting potential available to him in spiritual strength as given by the Holy Spirit, is a person who functions in even greater inner torment because his desire to be Christ-like is heightened by his repentance and trust in the Lord. But he does not yet have the equipment to handle this — he is not yet open to the fullness of the Holy Spirit.

I agree with those who hold to the third option. I believe it is the one supported by the most convincing evidence from the text itself and leads you and me on to what ultimately is the healthiest understanding of the Christian life. I believe that those who describe a "life in the Spirit" void of any struggle with the "old nature," "the flesh," are describing the Christian life in terms that are not true to our human situation.

The biblical scholar F. F. Bruce emphasizes that this is no abstract argument but is rather the very echo of Paul's personal experience. He knows what it is to be torn apart in a spiritual struggle. John Calvin and Martin Luther share in holding to this third option. Calvin goes so far as to argue that this conflict of which the apostle Paul speaks does not exist in a person before he is renewed by the Spirit of God. "For regeneration only begins in this life; the relics of the flesh which remain, always follow their own corrupt propensities, and thus carry on a contest against the Spirit."

Martin Luther comes to the same conclusion. He states that saints, at the same time as they are righteous, are also sinners. They are like sick men under the care of a physician. In fact, they are sick; but healthy in the hope and in the fact that they are beginning to be healthy. He says, "They are people for whom the worst possible thing is the presumption that they are healthy, because they suffer a worse relapse."

It's important to integrate Paul's teaching. We need to bring together this divinely revealed understanding that we've seen in chapters 6 and 7, that the Christian is one who has been given life and freedom in Jesus Christ. We have been baptized with Christ, going through His death and His resurrection. We are redeemed by His grace. We are people who not only claim that we're new creatures in Christ, we also admit to an inner battle that comes at the very place where our life comes into conflict with God's will and with the world's standards. Martin Luther talks about a bondage that is as deadening as sin itself, a tyranny called the "presumption that I am flawless."

Paul is distinguishing between the theoretical and the

practical when it comes to the theme of victory in the Christian life. Remember, now he's talking about sanctification. He's addressing what he has to say to believers — not to unbelievers. Try to capture the distinction with me.

Romans, in chapter 6 and the first part of chapter 7, deals with the theoretical. You and I are positionally right before God. You and I are alive to God and dead to sin. We are clothed in his righteousness. We are headed for heaven. We are made perfect by him. We have eternal security. You and I can stake our lives on this fact. This is the theoretical.

Now we come to the practical. You and I have an old nature at war with a new nature. The person that Paul is describing in the latter part of chapter seven is not a person who has never known Christ, nor a person who knows Christ but has not experienced sanctification. The person that Paul is describing at this point is himself. You and I can be very grateful for Paul's honesty at this point. He describes his own actions in the bluntest terms possible: "I do not understand my own actions. For I do not do what I want, but I do the very thing I hate" (Romans 7:15b).

Although the war has been won, the battle continues. The big contest is over. Satan knows he has lost — but he still can make it pretty uncomfortable for you and for me. We have a nature that is in bondage to sin which is in the process of being changed into a new nature. God treats us as if we had never sinned on the basis of Christ's work on the cross. At the same time, He continues to work in us through the gradual maturing process of sanctification, which is never fully completed in this life. It is only completed when we've passed from this life into a glorified existence with Jesus Christ in eternity.

This old nature explains the struggle that you and I have

living the Christian life. Each of us has what Robert Louis Stevenson labeled in his great novel the Dr. Jekyll and the Mr. Hyde living inside of us. We are two personalities. There's a kind of spiritual schizophrenia. On the one hand, we desire the things of Christ. On the other hand, we're in this inner cosmic battle with Satan, in which the things of the world look so appealing. We're citizens of two worlds. We may sing our hymns, saying "that this world is not my home, I'm just passing through," but we still are in this world. We struggle with the temptations of this world. That's what John Bunyan wrote about in *Pilgrim's Progress*. We're pulled two ways on our journey to the Celestial City. On the one hand, we know the promises of God and all that He has done for us, both in this life and the next. Yet, there's that old nature that keeps whispering to us, "Turn around, go back. The struggle isn't worth it. The temptations and the testings of the journey are to no profit."

Some stand and preach saying that once Paul came to faith in Jesus Christ, he never again struggled with sin. Wouldn't it be nice to say this? They say it was the old Paul in Romans 7. It's the new Paul in Romans 8. But wait a moment. Would it be so nice to be able to say that? Paul was gutsy in his candor. To try to say anything else is heresy. He shares his experience with you to encourage you. Take comfort from his words:

> So I find it to be a law that when I want to do right, evil lies close at hand. For I delight in the law of God, in my inmost self, but I see in my members another law at war with the law of my mind and making me captive to the law of sin which dwells in my members. Wretched man that I am! Who will deliver me from this body of death? (Romans 7:21-24).

If Paul had this kind of a struggle, don't be surprised that you do too. There were even points in his life when he was suicidal, wanting to be freed from the spiritual and physical limitations of his life. At the same time, he could say, "Thanks be to God through Jesus Christ our Lord! So then, I of myself serve the law of God with my mind, but with my flesh I serve the law of sin" (Romans 7:25).

There's a curse that comes from emphasizing the theoretical teaching about the new life we have in Jesus Christ without dealing with the practical, down-to-earth dynamics of the Christian life. On one occasion I was sharing a conference platform with a speaker who was telling how there was a different Paul in Romans 7 from the one in chapter 8. This speaker was talking about living the totally victorious Christian life. He described entering into full sanctification as if it has happened once for all. Yet, I noticed that he was pretty tough on his wife and others. He was unbelievably critical of other ministers. He had blinders on. He couldn't acknowledge the very struggle of his own life because he had been taught that once you were sanctified, you're freed from the struggle with your old nature.

The bottom line is that we are split personalities. We dare not ignore it. We continue to have tremendous potential for destructive as well as constructive activity. Our lives are in a civil war. We need help. God has given us the theology that equips us both to fight the battle and to receive the help.

Actually, what Paul has done by telling us his own experience has been to give us a three-point survival kit that will help us in the struggle. Some of us are so perfectionistic in our bent that we despair of our failures in the Christian life. Paul says go ahead and declare three statements about yourself to take you off this perfectionistic treadmill:

First, feel free to say, "I don't understand." I don't understand when I work so hard at a marriage that it doesn't go better. I don't understand physical pain and the weakness in my life. I don't understand why, when I try to do the right thing, I do the wrong. That's what Paul says in verse fifteen, "I don't understand my own actions."

Second, feel free to say, "As hard as I try, I'm never going to be perfect in this life." Paul said it in verse eighteen, "For I know that nothing good dwells within me, that is, in my flesh." Leave yourself a little room for failure. That's what Paul's talking about. Churches ought to have testimony services that don't concentrate just on victory but talk a little about failure. Jesus has given you the room for some failure.

Finally, feel free to say, "God, here's how I really feel about myself and about you." That's what Paul did in verse twenty-four, "Wretched man that I am!" God's interested in you being real. Tell him what you're thinking. Get it off your chest. He can handle it. There's no greater catharsis than to honestly be yourself before God.

Freedom in the Spirit 13

There is therefore now no condemnation for those wo
are in Christ Jesus. For the law of the Spirit of life in
Christ Jesus has set me free from the law of sin and
death (Romans 8:1-2).

YOU AND I can thank God for Romans 7, because
it alerts us to the fact that the Christian life is a
struggle. We have the theory. We know about what God
has done for us. We know the ultimate outcome. That does
not free us from the reality of the cosmic battle that rages
within. Sometimes it is severe. Then there are times in
which life is more calm. Read the biographies of the great
men and women of the Christian faith and you will en-
counter stories that parallel the experience of Paul —
stories that parallel your own experience.

But hidden in this seventh chapter is a hint of something
yet to come. Paul follows his own admission of a sense of
"wretchedness" by saying, "Thanks be to God through
Jesus Christ our Lord!" (Romans 7:25). The pain and
anguish are great. But this is not the end of the story.
Already in this seventh chapter we have a hint of what is to
follow in the eighth chapter. Paul now introduces us to a
tremendous theme that will move us beyond the downbeat
of defeat into the possible reality of victory.

If we were left with a period at the end of chapter 7 we
would have every reason to be discouraged people. This
little hint of something to come is now followed by one of
the greatest chapters in the Bible. I'm not the only one to
make this evaluation. One Bible expositor sent a letter to
twenty prominent American expository preachers. He

asked them to imagine themselves shipwrecked on a desert island on which they would have access to only one chapter out of the entire Bible. "Which chapter would you want that to be?" With no previous prompting from him, six of the twenty chose Romans 8. Although we take great comfort in knowing the struggles of Paul, as revealed in Romans 7, we now experience the joy of knowing that there is something more than a life of continuous struggle that so often ends in defeat. If you and I try to be victorious on our own we are in trouble. There is a freedom from this incessant pull of the old nature. Paul confronts us with a positive message.

I

As Christians, you and I need to be reminded of what we can count on from God. It makes no difference how great our struggle has been, is, and will be. Here are three liberating facts that we can claim.

One. *You are eternally secure.* "There is therefore now no condemnation for those who are in Christ Jesus" (Romans 8:1).

Do you catch the significance of that statement? If you have repented of sin, if you have put your trust in Jesus Christ, you are "saved." Don't back off from using that word. Christ has given you salvation. You are saved. He has rescued you for eternity. At times, you may feel like a wretched person. You may feel battered by life's experiences. You may have failed many more times than you would have liked. But in God's eyes you are a very special person. You've seen Mr. Rogers on TV look directly into the eyes of your little ones, telling them, "You're special. I'm your friend. You're my neighbor." God, too, calls you by name. You're His friend. You're part of His neighborhood.

Two. *You are now a free person.* "For the law of the

Spirit of life in Christ Jesus has set me free from the law of sin and death" (Romans 8:2).

The war may rage, but the victory is certain. The old law of sin and death, as painful as it is in its death pangs, has been defeated by the law of the Spirit of life in Jesus Christ. You have been set free. Jesus moved into this world as a ransom for all of us held hostage by sin and death. Paul tells us that God sent His own Son to do what the law could not.

Three. *You are now positionally perfect.* "For God has done what the law, weakened by the flesh, could not do: sending his own Son in the likeness of sinful flesh and for sin, he condemned sin in the flesh, in order that the just requirement of the law might be fulfilled in us, who walk not according to the flesh but according to the Spirit" (Romans 8:3-4).

In God's eyes you are just as if you had never sinned. It's the result of what Christ has done for you. I don't care how big your struggle is. You may be in the very midst of Romans Seven, hating yourself for the fact that your Christian life at this moment is something far less than victorious. Although God is aware of your struggle, he does not see you as wretched. He identifies with your pain. His heart breaks as he identifies with your anguish. However, he sees you as one who is clothed in righteousness. You can take all of the graphic language of the Scriptures and apply it to yourself. He sees you as washed in the blood of the Lamb. He sees you as one made clean through the supreme sacrifice of Christ. Although you are painfully aware of your imperfection, He has labeled you perfect. Granted, you can grieve Him. You can break His heart. You can rebel as a child rebels against a loving parent. He may discipline you. He may do his best to encourage you to a renewed faithfulness. However, He never plays games with His love. He refuses to manipulate you by the turning off and on of His care. You are His. You are one of the family.

II

Paul now goes on to describe that yours can be a life of victory. You need not live with a perpetual sense of failure, the failure that comes when you struggle in your own power, without surrendering. A Christian life lived only in struggle, without surrender, is a miserable existence.

Paul describes, in the eighth chapter of Romans, a life of victory in which you live life in the Spirit, not in the flesh.

The life of ultimate alienation is that of one who doesn't have the Holy Spirit. We're talking about unregenerate man. We're talking about men and women who have never repented of sin, having trusted their lives to Jesus Christ. Having just shown us what God has done for those of us who have trusted in Jesus Christ, Paul reminds us of what our lives were before we came to Christ. They were marked by five characteristics.

First, we had a mind-set on the flesh. We were locked into one-dimensional living. This is not our situation as believers. We now live two-dimensional lives. That's why we feel the struggle when our old nature is in conflict with our new nature.

Second, we had our minds set toward death. We were in a downward spiral, on a collision course. Had God not reached down to touch us, our end would not have been a pleasant one.

Third, we had a mind-set that was hostile to God. What a terrible thought to think that we were once living in alienation from our Creator.

Fourth, our unregenerate hearts could not submit to God. We did our own thing, no matter how good or how bad that thing was. We were without righteousness, that position of perfection before God.

Finally, as unregenerate men we could not please God.

If you feel that this statement is a bit severe, let me read it directly from God's Word: "For those who live according to the flesh set their minds on the things of the flesh, but those who live according to the Spirit set their minds on the things of the Spirit. To set the mind on the flesh is death, but to set the mind on the Spirit is life and peace. For the mind that is set on the flesh is hostile to God; it does not submit to God's law, indeed it cannot; and those who are in the flesh cannot please God" (Romans 8:5-8).

Paul uses the word "flesh" often in his New Testament writings. One usage is quite literal. He speaks of bodily circumcision. Another usage is a more general expression that means "according to flesh." When he uses such a phrase, he means "looking at things from the human point of view." He talks about Abraham as being our forefather "according to the flesh." He's simply saying "humanly speaking."

But Paul has a third use of the word "flesh" that applies specifically in this chapter and in others. He talks about days when we believers were "in the flesh." He talks about those who "walk according to the flesh" as distinct from those who live the Christian life. When he speaks in these terms he is emphasizing the fact that those who are "in the flesh" cannot please God. He's emphasizing what we've already alluded to as one-dimensional living, living that is in bondage to sin. When Paul uses the word "flesh" in this way he really means human nature in all its weakness, all its impotence, all its helplessness. William Barclay refers to it as human nature in its vulnerability to sin and to temptation. Paul is referring to human nature apart from Christ, apart from God — everything that attaches you and me to the world instead of to God.

The flesh is the lower side of man's nature. Paul is not thinking exclusively of bodily or sexual sins when he gives a list of the works of the flesh in Galatians 5:19-21. He includes those sins but also talks about idolatry, hatred, wrath, strife, heresies, envy, and murder. This third usage of the word flesh is not physical. It is spiritual. The flesh is human nature in all its sin and weakness. Flesh is all that you and I are without God, without Christ.

Paul has woven into his description of the ultimate life of alienation, which marks unregenerate man, a description of your and my life as it is lived according to the Spirit. He talks about having a mind-set that is right: "Those who live according to the Spirit set their minds on the things of the Spirit" (Romans 8:5). Yours is a mind-set on an upward spiral. Yours is also a mind-set that is living in the reality of God's promise of life and peace. "But to set the mind on the Spirit is life and peace" (Romans 8:6).

Paul is making a distinct contrast between life lived in the flesh and life lived in the Spirit, between unregenerate man and regenerate man. He writes, "But you are not in the flesh, you are in the Spirit, if in fact the Spirit of God dwells in you. Any one who does not have the Spirit of Christ does not belong to him. But if Christ is in you, although your bodies are dead because of sin, your spirits are alive because of righteousness. If the Spirit of him who raised Jesus from the dead dwells in you, he who raised Christ Jesus from the dead will give life to your mortal bodies also through his Spirit which dwells in you" (Romans 8:9-11).

What Paul is trying to tell you and me is that we have a fantastic power within us. Granted, there's a struggle. Any life that is worth living has its struggle. Paul wants to remind you and me that even though there is the reality of struggle, you and I have available to us a power that is not available to unregenerate man. The Spirit of God dwells in you and me. The sooner you and I realize that we can't win the battle on our own, the more quickly we will have some of the benefits of the victorious life as described in Romans 8. The more we try to struggle along on our own, putting our own Christian lives together, piece by piece, the more we'll have the sense of failure in our day-to-day existence.

There are a couple of reasons why some of us have Christian lives marked by so much failure.

One reason is that some of us just don't realize that we have the Holy Spirit living in us. Don't believe anyone who tells you that the Holy Spirit comes into your life sometime later in a subsequent spiritual experience. Peter, on that day of Pentecost, declared, "Repent, and be baptized every one of you in the name of Jesus Christ for the forgiveness of your sins; and you shall receive the gift of the Holy Spirit." He's stating in his words what Paul has just told us. If you don't have the Spirit of Christ you simply don't belong to Jesus. If you do belong to Jesus you have the Holy Spirit residing in you. Don't ever forget it.

Another reason for our failure is some of us see the Holy Spirit as only a concept. It's a nice idea that has no practical relevance to our lives. We've never been gripped by the reality that the Holy Spirit is a person. Paul tells you and me that we are privileged to "walk not according to the flesh but according to the Spirit" (Romans 8:4). In verses 12, 13, and 14 he tells us, "So then, brethren, we are debtors, not to the flesh, to live according to the flesh — for if you live according to the flesh you will die, but if by the Spirit you put to death the deeds of the body you will live. For all who are led by the Spirit of God are sons of God." You and I are released to walk in the Spirit, to be led by the Spirit.

The problem for some of us is that we don't even know of the spiritual warfare going on within us. The Bible tells us that Satan yearns to control us. He tempts us by doing everything he can to pull us away from the Lord. And

there is the Holy Spirit who resides in us and does everything he can to help us live according to God's ways. If you
were to vote right now, I imagine that your vote would be
for God's ways. However, when we get back to living and
forget that we're engaged in this cosmic warfare, we live
defensively, failing to take the initiative. As long as we can
keep the enemy on the other side of the DMZ, we feel safe.
We're willing to live with a truce. Ours is a policy of
"containment." We think in terms of "peaceful coexist-
ence" with the enemy. We've forgotten the word victory.

There are many pictures I could use to describe this life
in the Spirit. It's more than a Sunday stroll. It involves
daily surrender to the Holy Spirit. It involves saying a
conscious "no" to the old life. It involves granting the
realistic nature of momentary defeats. Don't let them dig a
hole for you and bury you. You'll never be perfect in this
life. Your perfection is what Christ has given you. But on
the other hand, never let the enemy push you into full
retreat. This is why we're urged to be armed for our
warfare.

This struggle between flesh and the Spirit can be described by comparing it to two opposing elements in the
natural world. One is water. The other is fire. Water always seeks the lowest possible level that runs downhill.
Fire always seeks a higher level. Water will extinguish fire
and fire will evaporate water. You cannot have fire and
water in the same place. It's the same way with the flesh
and the Spirit. You cannot have them both in the same
place. Flesh, like water, goes down. The Spirit, like fire,
goes up.

Yet, there's an interesting fact. If you put water in a
kettle, the water will go to the bottom of the kettle. But if
you put the kettle over fire, the power of the fire will go
through the kettle into the water, and the water will rise
like fire. It goes up in steam. It acts just like fire. Why?
Because the power of the fire is in it. If that vapor mist gets

too far away from the fire and its heat, it will condense into droplets of water and fall to the ground. It will act as water did before.

This helps us understand people who have accepted Christ and for a while have walked with Him. Lives have been changed, filled with happiness and joy. Occasionally you'll see someone who has stopped walking with the Lord. They no longer read their Bibles or pray. They have no joy in the Lord. They begin to act exactly as they did before they accepted Christ. The problem is that as long as the power of the fire is there the water is lifted up and carried by the heat. But when we quench the Holy Spirit, when we throw cold water on His fire, we cool off and think and act very much as we used to think and act before we came to Christ.

Paul concludes this section of the eighth chapter by letting you know you are a child of God. He writes, "For you did not receive the spirit of slavery to fall back into fear, but you have received the spirit of sonship. When we cry, 'Abba, Father!' it is the Spirit himself bearing witness with our spirit that we are children of God, and if children, then heirs, heirs of God and fellow heirs with Christ, provided we suffer with him in order that we may also be glorified with him" (Romans 8:15-17).

What he's talking about is a personal relationship with God. He's talking about you submitting yourself to the authority of a loving, generous, caring Father. He's talking about you interacting with God on personal terms, yearning to walk daily in fellowship with Him. He's describing a relationship in which you trust Him and call Him Father in your sufferings, in your struggles, as well as in your victory.

The word "Abba" to the Hebrew meant more than "Father." It really meant "Daddy." It's what a child would say sitting on his father's knee.

Two years ago I was staying in the Jerusalem Hilton, a

brand new skyscraper hotel. One afternoon the elevator broke down. I stood waiting at one of the upper floors. I heard the pathetic cry of a distressed little boy stuck between floors on the elevator. He was crying "Abba! Abba!" The tone of his voice captured all the feeling and sentiment that is yours and mine as our life in the Spirit enables us to call out in our distress of struggle. "Daddy! Daddy!" And I'll never forget the reunion that came twenty or thirty minutes later when the elevator was once again working and that little Jewish lad emerged, freed from his mobile cell into the arms of his loving father — who had been there all the time.

Yours can be a life of freedom as you claim your heavenly Father's love and care through the struggles into the victory of life lived in the Spirit.

Spiritual Breathing 14

For all who are led by the Spirit of God are sons of
God (Romans 8:14).

DO YOU REMEMBER those days when Mount Everest in the Himalayas was still considered unconquerable? Expedition after expedition endeavored to scale its heights. There was loss of life. There were failed hopes. Exorbitant amounts of money were spent by persons who never realized their dreams.

There was a reconnaissance mission in 1921, followed by frustrated attempts in 1922, 1924, and 1933. There was another reconnaissance mission in 1935, followed by two more frustrated attempts in 1936 and 1938. Again, there was a reconnaissance mission in 1951, followed by the spring attempt of 1952 and the autumn attempt of 1952. Finally, in 1953, an expedition led by Colonel John Hunt made its multipronged attack on the summit. On May 29, 9:00 A.M., E. P. Hillary and his Sherpa guide, Tenzing, reached the 29,028 foot summit as the world stood in awe.

During those thirty years of futility there were technological advances in the development of the helicopter that could have made an assault on the summit much easier. However, to land on the top without going through the struggle would have minimized the victory. It would barely have received notice.

The eighth chapter of Romans is a biblical summit. To spiritually helicopter onto it, without having worked one's way through the first seven chapters, is to minimize what it means to understand God's gift of life in the Spirit. It's only as we understand the true nature of man, the amazing nature of God's grace, and the reality of struggle in the Christian life that we are privileged to fully appreciate the joy of what God has given us. He helps us reach the summit of our spiritual pilgrimage, no matter how rough the journey.

Some of us want instant success. We don't like pain. We can't relate to struggle. We've been raised on "TV dinners," in which everything is prepared by others and simply spoon-fed to us. We don't appreciate what it takes to provide good nutrition.

On the other hand, some of us get caught up in the struggle of living. We find life painful. We're aware of the ambiguity of our existence. We know that there are few easy answers. We are engaged in a spiritual warfare. We know that the forces of Satan are in mortal combat with the angelic hosts of God. We spend all of our time engaged in the battle. We have little sense of victory.

Take all these mixed metaphors and relate them to the conquest of Everest. We spend our lives spiritually engaged in reconnaissance missions and even an occasional expedition. But we never arrive at the top. We never scale the heights. How sad it is. Although God doesn't helicopter us to the top, He does help us get there. Through Him, you and I can conquer life. Our need not be a life of perpetual failure. Victory is possible.

How can this be? Because you, as one who has repented of sin and put your trust in Jesus Christ, have the Holy Spirit.

But you say, "I can't relate to that. The whole concept of the Trinity confuses me. Oh, some of it I can understand. When you talk about God, the Father, I can sense that there is a divine being who created and sustains this universe. When you talk about God, the Son, I can some-how relate to this God become man as I read the Scriptures and experience a personal relationship of forgiveness through what Christ has done on the cross. It's this business about the Holy Spirit that confuses me, especially that spooky language about a 'Holy Ghost.'"

The eighth chapter of Romans talks about a life that is lived with the fullness of the Holy Spirit. Paul states, "For all who are led by the Spirit of God are sons of God" (Romans 8:14). The Holy Spirit is not an *It*. The Holy Spirit is a *He*. The Holy Spirit is the personal One who is available to you.

The Holy Spirit was present at the creation and all through human history, prior to the day we call Pentecost. Acts, chapter 2, describes that special appearance of the Holy Spirit in the life of the early church. Today, we live in the potential fullness of the Holy Spirit. It is this coming reality that Paul writes about in Romans 8.

I

Here are some of the contributions that the Holy Spirit makes to you in Christ's world. Here are some of the ways in which He is manifested.

One manifestation of the Holy Spirit is a *strongly felt presence*.

Have you ever had moments of inspiration? Have you ever had the feeling that God was especially near to you? Those feelings come from the Holy Spirit. Granted, there are times that we can get false feelings of the nearness of God. Yet I think you and I know the difference. Our conscience and the Scriptures give us a healthy equilibrium. You know that you are not alone. You sense the presence of God. You have the "peace of God which passes all understanding, which keeps your heart and mind through Christ Jesus." Sometimes it comes even in the midst of the most confusing, troublesome circumstances. The Holy Spirit is *God with you.*

Another manifestation of the Holy Spirit is *power.*

Are you aware that the Holy Spirit is mentioned approximately 300 times in the New Testament? Almost always, He is associated with power. The Holy Spirit is the source of divine energy. The Holy Spirit is the source of spiritual electricity. It's important that you and I are plugged into this power. Even as Christians, we can try to motivate our own lives independent of that energy and find that we run out of fuel.

Another manifestation of the Holy Spirit is as *comforter.*

A comforter is one who wipes your tears away. A comforter is one who puts his arms around you, supporting you, when your strength is gone. This is not the only meaning of the word. The Holy Spirit is actually a "helper." He comes up alongside of you to enable you. The Holy Spirit is there urging you on. When you feel weak, call on Him for support.

Another manifestation of the Holy Spirit is *guidance.*

Do you listen for God's guidance? Do you have an open mind in which the clutter is swept away so that you can hear what God has to say? The Holy Spirit speaks through the Scriptures as you are willing to take time to read the Bible. He confronts you with what is new, what is unexpected, what is mandatory. If you sense the Holy Spirit is giving you instruction, it's important that you compare that instruction with what the Bible says. The Spirit is never at odds with Himself. "The Spirit never gives witness against the Spirit." He is consistent. He's loving. He's prepared to instruct you precisely when you need it.

The problem with many of us is that we've never given a direct answer to the question, "Do I really want God's will or my own?" We often tell God what we want, and we hope that He'll conform His will to our will. It's like a fellow telling God, "I'm going to marry Sandra. I hope you like the idea God, because I'm going to do it no matter what You think." Or, it's like the businessman who says, "I'm going to sell the business. I hope it works out okay and has God's blessing." The key to having the guidance of the Holy Spirit is to come to God before you make the decision.

The exciting fact is that when God wants to get something across to you, He has a way to do it. He gives guidance, but you and I must be listening. We must be living in what one might call "the stream of the Holy Spirit." It's amazing how much guidance we get when we are actively listening to what God has to say. By that I'm not suggesting that you're going to hear any great voice coming out of the sky. I'm talking about the sensitivity that is yours through God's instruction, by His Spirit, through the Scriptures and through the inner voice that captures the attention of the listening spiritual ear.

Another manifestation of the Holy Spirit is the *conviction of sin*.

This week I was privileged to stumble across an old recording by Samuel Shoemaker, for many years the rector of Calvary Episcopal Church in Pittsburgh. Sam Shoemaker, who was so instrumental in my call into the Christian ministry, was speaking about the Holy Spirit. He said that the Holy Spirit is not just "the Comforter," the Holy Spirit is also "the Discomforter." The Holy Spirit is in the life of the believer, alerting him to the fact that some things have to change. Anything that gets between you and God, and you and others, has to go. As for those long-standing resentments, let go of them. There are those self-indulgences that He wants to sort out, making you and me world Christians, not just narcissistic, self-centered, get-all-I-can-out-of-life, let-the-rest-of-the-world-go-to-hell kind of Christians. If you come to church on Sunday morning and find yourself agitated by the messages, check them out with the Scriptures. If what is being said is not in the Word of God, dismiss it. But, if you persist in that inner agitation, and you can't disprove what is being said by comparing it with the Scriptures, I suggest that you're experiencing a manifestation of the Holy Spirit. If you come up with a half-a-dozen reasons why you should not tithe, to the point that you're even angered by this emphasis, yet somehow you can't dismiss it from your mind, it's the Holy Spirit convicting you. You'll never be comfortable again until you either completely quench the Spirit, shutting Him out of your existence, or until you give in and obey.

Another manifestation of the Holy Spirit is *the way in which He uses you to bring faith in Jesus Christ to another person.*

Are you aware that God has chosen you to be the primary agent of evangelism? The church does not grow through every-member canvasses or slick Madison Avenue campaigns. It grows through the integrity of one beggar showing another beggar where he got bread. The only legitimate kind of church growth occurs when the Holy Spirit works through you to tell someone else about the grace of our Lord Jesus Christ. No one can come to Jesus Christ without the Holy Spirit being the energizing personality.

And, the Holy Spirit is manifested through *the unity and the fellowship that is ours as fellow believers in Jesus Christ.*

Wherever you have a few Christians together, there will be an undergirding sense of oneness which gives the assurance that we are family. The world is to know that we are Christians by our love. What a privilege.

I could go on and on giving additional manifestations of the Holy Spirit. I could do it in a much more theological way. I could take a concordance of the Bible and go right through the Scriptures, specifically isolating verses that talk about the Holy Spirit. But I want to strive now for some practical background that will open to you a greater understanding of what Paul is trying to tell us in Romans 8.

II

If you are a believer in Jesus Christ, you're forced to make a decision. You have to answer the question, "Who is the Lord of my life?"

Some of us see Jesus Christ as our Savior. We clutch that one-way ticket to heaven. We know that we are forgiven and have been promised life with Him beyond this life on earth. At the same time, we reserve the right to call all the shots in our own existence.

Campus Crusade for Christ has put out a little booklet titled, *Have You Made the Wonderful Discovery of the Spirit-Filled Life?* The booklet begins by stating that everyday can be an exciting adventure for the Christian who knows the reality of being filled with the Holy Spirit, and who lives moment-by-moment under His gracious control. Then it goes on to describe three kinds of persons.

One is labeled "natural man." The natural man sits on the throne of his own life. Jesus Christ is on the outside. The interests of this person's life are controlled by self, often resulting in discord and frustration. This person has not received Jesus Christ as Savior.

Two is "spiritual man." This is one who is controlled and empowered by the Holy Spirit. This person has received Christ. Whereas the natural man lives a self-controlled life, this person is living a Christ-controlled life. Christ sits on the throne of the life. The self is dethroned. All of the interests of this person's life are under the control of the infinite God, resulting in harmony with God's plan.

Three is "carnal man." This is a person who has received Jesus Christ as Savior but who lives in defeat because he trusts his own efforts to live the Christian life. This is a self-controlled life. Christ is within the circle of this person's life. But instead of sitting on the throne, Christ is dethroned and ego, or "finite self," is back on the throne. The interests of this person's life are controlled by self, often resulting in discord and frustration.

The spiritual person has some personal traits that come about as a result of trusting God. His life is Christ-centered. It's empowered by the Holy Spirit. He introduces others to Christ. He has an effective prayer life. He understands God's Word. He trusts God. He obeys God. He begins to experience some of the fruits of the Spirit such as love, joy, peace, patience, kindness, faithfulness, and goodness. The degree to which these traits are manifested in the life depends upon the extent to which the Christian trusts the Lord with every detail of his life. One who is only beginning to understand the ministry of the Holy Spirit should not be discouraged if he's not as fruitful as more mature Christians who have known and experienced this truth for a longer period.

All of this raises a question. Why is it that most Christians are not experiencing the abundant life? The main reason is that the carnal person trusts in his own efforts to live the Christian life. He is either uninformed about or has forgotten about God's love, forgiveness, and power. He has an up-and-down spiritual experience. He can't understand himself. He wants to do what is right, but he can't do it. He fails to draw upon the power of the Holy Spirit to live the Christian life. He has an ignorance of his spiritual heritage. Unbelief creeps in. Disobedience marks his existence. There's a loss of love for God and for others. There's a poor prayer life. There's no desire to study the Bible. His life may be marked by a legalistic attitude, impure thoughts, jealousy, guilt, worry, discouragement, a critical spirit, frustration, aimlessness.

How do you relate to all of this? Which of these persons are you? Who is sitting on the throne of your life? Are you there? Is Christ there? If you're sitting there, I'll guarantee you one thing. Your life is not one in which you are walking in the fullness of the Holy Spirit. Certainly if you've repented of sin, you have your ticket to heaven. But frankly, if that's all there is, it's one "hell" of an existence. You're on the train, but you're traveling third or fourth class — when you're privileged to have a "first class" existence.

The lives of people who have conquered the spiritual Everest have been marked by struggle. They have gone through some of the anguish the apostle Paul describes in chapter seven. There is always a degree of this warfare going on. However, if you study their lives carefully, you will find that this struggle, which is subsequent to salvation, is followed by an additional surrender in which they run up the white flag, allowing Jesus Christ to be Lord, voluntarily turning the throne over to Him.

That's what the songwriter was trying to say in those words "Trust and obey/For there's no other way/To be happy in Jesus/But to trust and obey."

That's what Dr. Robert Boyd Munger was trying to say in his little booklet, *My Heart, Christ's Home*, as he describes the nonbeliever as someone for whom Christ is on the outside knocking, wanting entrance. Then he tells about the believer who has allowed Christ into his house but has offered Him a chair in the front hallway, where the Lord sits. Dressed in His overcoat and holding His hat in His hand, the Lord waits minutes, then hours, then days, then even years to have access to the rest of the house — while the host carries on business as usual.

I came to faith in Jesus Christ as a young boy. At that

point I received my ticket to heaven. I received God's grace, freely given. That was about all there was to my Christian life. I went to church. I went through the motions. I tried to read my Bible regularly. I tried to pray frequently. However, Jesus Christ was only my Savior — he was not my Lord. It was only through some crushing experiences that I came to the realization that I needed to be under new management. I needed more than a Savior. I needed in addition, a Lord, a Master. I'll never forget that cold, northern Illinois, winter night as I paced back and forth across that football practice field under the black sky studded with stars. I was engaged in an inner battle, wanting to let go, yet wanting to hold on. I wanted to map my own career, choose my own wife, make the primary decisions of my own life, to do with my sexuality what I wanted to do with it. Finally I came to the point, as I ran up the white flag, and said to the Lord, "I'm willing to come under new management. From now on, you're in charge. I'm going to live my life according to your Word as best I can."

I'd like to say that ever since then I've lived completely controlled by the Holy Spirit. Frankly, every so often I crawl right back up on the throne and knock the Lord off. And when I do it I pay the price. Yes, I'm still a Christian. God doesn't want you and me to be "just Christians." He wants you and me to live in the fullness of His Holy Spirit.

He wants you to be engaged in a practice called "spiritual breathing." If you become aware of an area of your life, an attitude, or an action that is displeasing to the Lord (even though you're walking with Him and sincerely desiring to serve Him), simply thank God that He's forgiven your sin — past, present, and future. On the basis of Christ's death on the cross, claim His love and forgiveness by faith and continue to fellowship with Him. If you retake the throne of your life through sin, a definite act of disobedience, breathe spiritually. Spiritual breathing is an exercise in faith. It enables you to continue to experience God's love and forgiveness. It involves exhaling the impure and inhaling the pure.

In exhaling, you confess your sin. Agree with God that it is sin, and thank him for His forgiveness. This involves repentance, a change in attitude and action, as you claim His promise: "If we confess our sins, he is faithful and just, and will forgive our sins and cleanse us from all unrighteousness" (1 John 1:9).

Spiritual breathing involves inhaling, surrendering the control of your life to Christ, appropriating the fullness of the Holy Spirit by faith. That's what the apostle Paul is talking about in Romans 8. He tells you and me to "walk not according to the flesh, but according to the Spirit," or "live according to the Spirit," or "to set the mind on the Spirit," or to be "led by the Spirit."

You are God's child. You can call him "Daddy." He wants to take care of you, and He has given you the gift of His Spirit to energize you, to motivate you. Take Him at His word.

From Temporary Hope to Ultimate Reality! 15

I consider that the sufferings of this present time are not worth comparing with the glory that is to be revealed to us (Romans 8:18).

YOU AND I are living in crises times.

We sense it as we read the newspaper headlines describing the economic recession into which our nation has plunged. A quarter of a million of our workers have been laid off in the automotive industry. Home building is at a standstill. The prime interest rate flutters between 18 and 20 percent. The economy doesn't look too promising.

The American family isn't in the best of shape. I could quote elaborate statistics describing the breakdown of marriage. I could describe, at quite some length, the kinds of conversations I've had with husbands and wives who basically love each other but can't seem to get along. Divorce is epidemic. Dreams are shattered, as children look on in wide-eyed bewilderment wondering what's happening to Mommy and Daddy. The best received films of the last year dealt with domestic problems.

The world is filled with refugees. We read of boat people. We try to help those from Southeast Asia. At the same time, we forget the Arab refugees in the Middle East, the starving nomads of Central Africa, the Afghan hordes that have fled to the border of Pakistan, and the Cubans who are doing their best to escape the communist regime of Castro.

I

Our world is in crisis. You and I have difficulties. Suffering is a reality.

One of the things I most appreciate about the Bible is its honest grappling with reality. God has given us His word; it's an honest Word. It doesn't put a sugar coating on life. Jesus said, "In this world you will have trouble." That's not the kind of statement most pastors talk about. We'd rather talk about things the way we'd like them to be than the way they actually are.

If you are a believer in Jesus Christ, you are automatically guaranteed some sufferings that are unique. Paul writes, "I consider that the sufferings of this present time are not worth comparing with the glory that is to be revealed to us" (Romans 8:18). You have sufferings in this present time. Some of them are brought about because you love Jesus Christ.

I was recently talking to a couple who were having financial problems because the husband's income has gone to half of what it was before he became a Christian. Prior to accepting Christ, he had been a bartender. He had no struggles of conscience about a profession he now sees as contrary to the will of God for him. He and his wife are having to adjust themselves to a whole new set of economic realities brought about, at least partially, by his trust in the Lord.

There are things worth more than an endeavor to avoid immediate pain and discomfort. Are you aware of that? Some of us would like to live lives free from struggle, free from suffering.

Last night, I finished reading Yigael Yadin's great book, titled *Masada*. This Israeli archaeologist and military and political leader recently excavated the Judean desert rock-fortress of Herod the Great. This stronghold overlooking the Dead Sea was the site on which Herod erected some of his most daring buildings, and also the scene of one of the most dramatic episodes in human history. The Romans had used their military power to crush a Jewish revolt. The predictions of Jesus, some forty years before, had been fulfilled when Titus destroyed the temple in A.D. 70. He stripped the Mount of Olives of its vegetation. He leveled the rest of Jerusalem, punishing the Jews for their insolence.

A number of the Jewish zealots retreated to the mountaintop fortress of Masada. There, for three years, they held out against the Romans. Finally, the Roman siege took its toll. The end was near. The suffering of these people was acute. They knew their hated enemy, the Romans, was finally ready to scale the heights. Under the leadership of Eleazar, they determined that whatever sufferings they had gone through were worth it. To surrender to the Romans would be the ultimate betrayal of all they believed in and stood for. These 960 survivors were challenged by Eleazar to die at their own hands rather than to surrender to the pagan Romans.

The Jewish historian Josephus describes husbands tenderly embracing their wives and taking their children into their arms. They gave each other long, parting kisses, as tears streamed down their faces:

Miserable men indeed were they! Whose distress forced them to slay their own wives and children with their own hands, as the lightest of those evils that were before them. So they not being able to bear the grief they were under for what they had done, any longer, and esteeming it an injury to those they had slain, to live even the shortest space of time after them — they presently laid all they had in a heap and set fire to it. They then chose ten men by lot out of them, to slay all the rest; every one of whom laid himself down by his wife and children on the ground, and threw his arms about them, and they offered their necks to the stroke of those who by lot executed that melancholy office; and when these ten had, without fear, slain them all, they made the same rule for casting lots for themselves, that the one whose lot it was should first kill the other nine, and after all, should kill himself. Accordingly, all those had courage sufficient to be no way behind one another, in doing or suffering; so, for a conclusion, the nine offered their necks to the executioner, and he who was the last of all, took a view of all the other bodies, lest perchance some or other among so many that were slain should want his assistance to be quite dispatched; and when he perceived that they were all slain, he set fire to the palace, and with the great force of his hand ran his sword entirely through himself, and fell down dead near to his own relations. So these people died with this intention, that they would not have so much as one soul among them all alive to be subject to the Romans.

Two women and five children huddled in a nearby cave aware of what was going on. The Romans found them. It was from their lips that they received the report as to how the 953 bodies happened to be lying there, dead at their own hands. There was still plenty of food and water. I'll not make a moral judgment encouraging any kind of suicide. However, even the Romans stood in awe of a people for whom certain values were worth more than any endeavor to avoid immediate pain and discomfort.

Paul is trying to tell us the same thing. Suffering is a reality. Sufferings, as tough as they are, are not final. There are things worth more than an endeavor to avoid immediate pain and discomfort. In fact, you and I as Christians are called to share in Christ's suffering. The apostle Paul puts it bluntly in his letter to the church at Philippi when he writes, "That I may know him and the power of his resurrection, and may share his sufferings, becoming like him in his death, that if possible I may attain the resurrection from the dead" (Philippians 3:10-11).

Dr. Charles Malik, professor emeritus of philosophy at the American University of Beirut, was one of the founders of the United Nations. He became president of the United Nations' 13th general assembly. He has served Lebanon politically as minister of foreign affairs, minister of national education and fine arts, and as a member of parliament. This brilliant, Christian citizen of world renown recently addressed a gathering in Newport Beach, the town in which I live. In his address he mused on the kind of leader our nation needs. He talked about the essential nature of suffering, saying that no one is prepared to give primary leadership until he has willingly involved himself in heartbreaking, painful suffering. He called for a leader who is "a man of sorrows and acquainted with grief."

So we shy away from suffering. We yearn to live antiseptic existences. We don't want to hurt. We avoid it at all costs. We fly in the face of the statement by that man of God, A. W. Tozer: "It is doubtful that God can use anyone greatly until He has hurt him deeply."

When you stop and think about one of the greatest leaders this world has ever seen, this message takes on all the more significance. His name was Moses. He spent forty years with all of the trappings of power in Pharoah's court. He spent another forty years on the back side of the desert, feeling like a loser, tending sheep. It was only out of these two contradictory experiences that there came that fusion which gave him the political understandings that could set his people free, and the knowledge of the Sinai desert that enabled him to lead the nation of Israel through their forty-year Exodus out of Egypt into the Promised Land.

All this talk about suffering finds its encapsuled statement in Romans 8:18: "I consider that the sufferings of this present time are not worth comparing with the glory that is to be revealed to us." So we whimper and complain about the sufferings of this moment, forgetting that there's a larger game plan. God is in charge. If we suffer with Christ, we will be glorified with Him. Today's suffering is temporary compared to eternity in the presence of Jesus Christ. You've got problems now. Look at them in the long haul — not only of the good that they produce but the fact that they are only temporary. You are in the process of preparing for glory.

II

You and I live in a period of expectant groaning.

Don't be surprised at the upheaval you are now experiencing in this world. It all makes sense. You've been told that it will be this way. The groaning of this present time points to the ultimate glory of the future.

The apostle Paul relates all this to nature. He lets us know that there are four basic principles involved which show us that we live in an era of painful, agonizing groanings.

Principle one: This groaning is temporary. Paul writes, "For the creation waits with eager longing for the revealing of the sons of God" (Romans 8:19). Everything will someday be restored to what it was. The pain that you experience. The upheaval of world conditions. The very nature of destructive elements that are part of nature, the hurricane, the earthquake, the drought, shall all be brought under control. All of these natural phenomena are of a temporary nature. I love the way J.B. Phillips translates verse 19. He says, "The whole creation is on tiptoe to see the wonderful sight of the sons of God coming into their own."

Principle two: This groaning is the consequence of the fall. Paul writes, "For the creation was subjected to futility, not of its own will but by the will of him who subjected it in hope" (Romans 8:20). This goes all the way back to the early verses of Genesis. Remember the perfection of God's creation? He looks at everything that He had created and declares, "It is good!" But then the story changes. Adam and Eve have been given freedom. In this freedom they can obey. In this freedom they can disobey. They have chosen to disobey. Then comes this painful word from God (Genesis 3:17-19):

> And to Adam he said,
> Because you have listened to the voice of your wife, and have eaten of the tree of which I commanded you, 'You shall not eat of it,' cursed is the ground because of you; in toil you shall eat of it all the days of your life; thorns and thistles it shall bring forth to you; and you shall eat the plants of the field. In the sweat of your face you shall eat bread till you return to the ground, for out of it you were taken; you are dust and to dust you shall return.

The very ground itself is victim of this frustration. Sin has bludgeoned all creation. It has taken its toll. The distortions of this world result from the fall.

Principle three: This groaning is a means to an end. Paul writes, "Because the creation itself will be set free from its bondage to decay and obtain the glorious liberty of the children of God" (Romans 8:21). A day is coming when all this creation will be set free. This is the bottom-line message of the book of Revelation. That's why there is such a blessing involved in this book. This is what the Bible refers to when it talks about a new heaven and a new earth. No longer will there be death. No longer will there be tears. No longer will there be mourning. No longer will there be division in the family. A new age will be ushered in when Jesus Christ returns to set up His new kingdom. All nature, all creation will bow humbly before the King of kings.

Principle four: This groaning is universal. Paul writes,

"And not only the creation, but we ourselves, who have the first fruits of the Spirit, groan inwardly as we wait for adoption as sons, the redemption of our bodies" (Romans 8:23).

All of creation is going through the pains of childbirth. The anguish you and I feel is natural to this birth process as a new order will be ushered in. Childbirth is painful. Women know what that pain is. I've sat by the hour with Anne as she's gone through labor with our three children. For the last two I was privileged to be with her right through the delivery. No, I've not felt the pain myself. But I've gone through the experience vicariously. I've seen on her face the agony of birth. I've also witnessed her ecstasy in delivery. I'll never forget those two occasions in which she, right through the whole process, refused any kind of anesthetic because she wanted to experience everything without anything dulling the pain. Each time, I watched her as she made the transition from excruciating pain to the exquisite joy of giving birth. I listened as she whispered, "It was worth it all."

You and I are part of a process, the process of groaning, of struggle, of pain, of travail. You and I are part of all creation as it is going through the birth pangs which, when we look back from that new order, will make it all worthwhile.

So, what do we do in the meantime? The apostle suggests three gifts that God has given to us.

First, He gives us hope. "For in this hope we were saved. Now hope that is seen is not hope. For who hopes for what he sees?" (Romans 8:24).

There are pessimists who see this world plunging toward ultimate disaster. They have no hope. H.G. Wells once said, "Man, who began in a cave behind a windbreak, will end in the disease soaked ruins of a slum." As Barclay observed, however, that was not the view of Paul.

He saw man's sin. He observed the state of the world. But also he saw God's redeeming power, so life was not a hopeless waiting for an inevitable end in a world full of sin and death. Paul looked forward to a liberation, a recreation brought about by the power of God.

Second, God not only gives us the gift of hope, He also enables us to wait with patience. "But if we hope for what we do not see, we wait for it with patience" (Romans 8:25). I believe that Barclay's translation of this paints a more adequate picture. He talks about us waiting with "eager expectation." As Barclay points out, the word in the Greek describes the attitude of a man who scans the horizon, searching the distance for the first signs of dawn. To Paul, life was not merely anxious waiting. Life was a thrilling anticipation. You and I are engaged in the battle with our own evil human nature. We live in this world, with all its problems. Nonetheless, the Christian does not only live in the world, but he also stands with strength and patience in expectation of the coming day of the Lord. Despair if you like — or optimistically anticipate Christ's victory.

Third, God gives you the gift of the Holy Spirit to help you live beyond yourself. Read these words of promise: "Likewise the Spirit helps us in our weakness; for we do not know how to pray as we ought, but the Spirit himself intercedes for us with sighs too deep for words. And he who searches the hearts of men knows what is the mind of the Spirit, because the Spirit intercedes for the saints according to the will of God" (Romans 8:26-27). Have you ever come to a point in your Christian life in which you don't know how you should pray? I've been there many times. The pain, the anguish is such that we find ourselves incapable of articulate expression. This passage tells us not only does all creation groan, not only do you and I groan, but the Holy Spirit also groans, making intercession for us. He takes those deep, inarticulate yearnings and transforms them into specific prayers that reach to the heart of God.

What Paul is saying is that you should not be surprised that you've got problems now. Look at the long haul. God has warned us that we live in a period of expectant groaning. All creation is involved in it. In the meantime, have hope. Wait with eager expectation. Remember that the very God of all creation is in tune with you as you allow His Holy Spirit to articulate for you your deepest needs. No death of a loved one, no broken home, no loss of prestige or position can take away this Spirit from you. Thanks be to God who giveth us the victory through Jesus Christ our Lord.

Do All Things Work Together for Good? 16

We know that in everything God works for good with those who love him, who are called according to his purpose (Romans 8:28).

THE BIBLE SAYS, "All things work together for good." We blithely reaffirm ourselves and others with this statement when things don't go our way.

"Do all things really work together for good?" wept the questioning young Marine whose patrol had been ambushed by the Viet Cong. He stood there exhausted and caked with dirt. Tears mingled with sweat dripped down his face onto his fatigues as he viewed the lifeless bodies of his friends stacked in front of him like cordwood. Now, years later, he lies in a California Veterans Hospital, a disfigured amputee.

"Do all things really work together for good?" muses a pretty young mother on a Braniff flight from Denver to Dallas. She glances sideways at her eight-year-old son, Timmy. He sits there contentedly, clutching his football autographed by the players of the Los Angeles Rams. His mother knows he also holds within his body that lethal disease, leukemia. Apart from a miracle, it will snuff out his radiant little life.

"Do all things really work together for good?" questions the doctor as he interviews Ralphie, a 12-year-old, 60-pound wisp of a boy "barely four feet tall, with gentle eyes and pale arms so thin it is almost impossible to believe that they could take a needle." Ralphie is a junkie, addicted to heroin. He is seriously ill with hepatitis, contracted from a dirty needle he used to mainline heroin, injecting it into a vein in his arm.

I

The Bible says that "all things work together for good." What many people fail to realize is that this enormous statement is not a reiteration of a "grin and bear it" Stoic philosophy. It is the affirmation of an absolute, total faith in a crucified and risen Lord. The apostle Paul burst free from the philosophic fatalism of his day that said "whatever will be will be" to affirm, with a radiance of expression, these words: "And we know that all things work together for good to them that love God, to them who are the called according to his purpose" (Romans 8:28).

One day a group of us were talking about this verse of Scripture at a men's Bible study. The question was raised, "What is the proper definition of 'good'?" For about fifteen minutes, the twenty-one men who were gathered around that table wrestled with this question, "What is good?" Initially, we defined it in terms of events and things. When I say that good things are happening to me, I tend to mean that things are going my way. I like what is going on. I am finding gratification from these events. When I receive something good, I find a security in that thing — whether it be money, prestige, power, popularity, a job, a car, or furnishings for the home.

Then we began to shift gears — to realize that this is not at all what Paul is talking about. Paul is saying something different. Good is not defined by events and things. It must be defined from a spiritual perspective — a kind of position from which we view all of life. Paul says all things work together for good. This is a clear statement. But it must not be viewed from a worldly perspective. The Christian life is no cornucopia of every physical and personal delicacy you may desire. To get in stride with the good that Paul talks about, you must be in stride with the God of eternity, realizing the transient, temporary nature of the life you are now living. Bishop Anders Nygren of Sweden writes:

> Just as the present aeon is to be followed by an eternity, it has already been preceded by an eternity. Only when we see our present existence set in God's activity, which goes from eternity to eternity, do we get it in right perspective. Then man comes to see that *everything* that comes to the Christian in this life — and consequently the sufferings of the present, too — must work together for good for him.

Paul is writing out of the experience of tremendous suffering. His life had not been easy. He had been in and out of prison. On five different occasions he had been whipped — receiving thirty-nine stripes. Three times he was beaten with rods. Once he was stoned. Three times he was shipwrecked. Often he had been imperiled by robbers and near drownings. Many times he was weary, in pain, hungry, thirsty, cold, and naked. All of this was done for Jesus Christ. All of this could have been avoided if he had taken the easy way.

But he didn't:

> Not that I speak in respect of want, for I have learned in whatsoever state I am in therewith to be content. I know both how to be abased, and I know how to abound: everywhere, and in all things, I am instructed both to be full and to be hungry; both to abound and to suffer need. I can do all things through Christ, which strengtheneth me (Philippians 4:11-13, KJV).

Paul sees the sufferings of this world from the perspective of the eternal. In spite of the difficulty he had come through, he could boldly say, "And we know that all things work together for good."

This good that Paul writes about is a commitment of life to the sovereign will of God. In fact, the primary emphasis of this text is an emphatic statement of the sovereignty of God in the past, in the future, and in the present. That which baffles us most when we lament our human condition is the fallibility of human wisdom. You and I spend so much of our time trying to reason things out, and only come to a dead end. The philosopher Seneca expressed this tendency so well when he wrote, "We fail to know what is necessary, because we study unnecessary things: indeed, we do not know what is good for us, because we study merely what injures us."

What this all boils down to is unbelief in the sovereignty of God. If God is on the throne, your life can be marked by confident living. You will see a good that goes beyond your own limited understanding. This is what faith is. The unbeliever in God wants his own values, not God's, to be supreme. If you are not experiencing a sense that all things are working together for good, you are simply not trusting Jesus Christ. You are trying to be your own God. Martin Luther, in his commentary on Romans, wrote, "The proud [unbelievers] desire to be like God. They want to place their thoughts not under God, but next to His, just as though they were perfect [as God is]. But that is much less possible than for the clay to tell the potter into what shape he should form it."

The life of faith covers every single situation. Your endeavor to explain everything, establishing your own sense of well-being, will only throw all of life out of kilter. The affirmation comes at the point that you trust this sovereign God who created you, sustains you, and offers you salvation through His incarnation, and redemption in the person of Jesus Christ.

II

Let's look at the second half of Romans 8:28. It reads, "With those who love him, who are called according to his purpose."

There are two conditions that must be met if you are to live in the reality of all things working together for good.

Condition One is captured in the phrase "with those who love him." I have heard this optimistic assurance that all things work together for good bantered about by non-Christians. If you have not given your life to Jesus Christ in faith, you cannot make this claim. This promise is not designed for you.

I will guarantee that if you are resisting a complete surrender of your life to Jesus Christ, you are either speeding toward a head-on collision with spiritual disaster, or you are inoculating yourself with a religious narcotic that gives you a false sense of well-being. All things do not work together for good when there is unconfessed sin in your life that blocks the free flow of God's Spirit. No, all things do not work together for good when you are exposing yourself to habits of life that run counter to God's biblical commands.

Don't for a moment expect to feel good about the life you are living if you are experimenting with chemical substances that are producing in you a euphoria that ultimately can destroy your body and mind. Your body is the temple of the Holy Spirit. If you think you can play with drugs and not get burned, you're a fool. I'd like to take you with me to the psychiatric hospital ward and let you talk with dozens of people who thought they could play with "grass," but found it only led to things that have caused them to destroy their minds. It breaks my heart to talk with people of all ages who admit their need, but when confronted with the dictates of God's Word, will not let go of sin. Some of the biggest problems facing people that I have counseled are the manifestations of rebellion against God in the improper use of drugs, the excessive use of alcohol, and the use of pre-marital or extramarital sex. One of these things, or something else, may be destroying you as you clutch it, loving it more than Jesus Christ. For some, selfishness, pride, judgmental attitudes, and thoughtlessness all work against meeting Condition One.

Are we willing to expose ourselves to the hurts of others or do we selfishly bottle ourselves up in self-centered living? His will is for us to go into His world with His care and message of redemption. Will we isolate ourselves from the pain and hurts of a bleeding world, egotistically trying to anesthetize ourselves from the world's anguish?

"All things work together for good to those that love God." What does it mean to love God? Listen to what Christ had to say: "He that hath my commandments and keepeth them, he it is that loveth me, and he that loveth me shall be loved of my father, and I will love him and manifest myself to him" (John 14:21, KJV).

Loving God involves surrender of your life to Him in the discipline of obedience. If you really love Jesus Christ, you will want to be caught up in His will. You will have a hunger to know more about Him. You will discard your disbelief. Your doubts will gradually crumble by the wayside as you let Him take over, making the ultimate expression of love by surrendering your will to His.

There is another condition of experiencing God's will for your life. Condition Two is encapsuled in the phrase, "to them who are the called according to his purpose."

What does it mean to be called according to the purpose of God? This phrase of the apostle Paul simply sets the priority straight. It points out that God is the initiator of your salvation — not you. Seldom does the Scripture talk about your love for God. All through the Bible there is reference to God's love for you. His call to you is an invitation. All you need to do is respond to it.

This condition of being called according to the purpose of God introduces one of the most difficult themes in Christian theology — the overlapping doctrines of divine foreknowledge, election, and predestination. It would be impossible to adequately deal with these doctrines in one book, except to say that your assurance of all things working together for good is not based on anything that you personally have done — but based on God's free gift of grace in Jesus Christ.

"But you said I'm to receive Jesus Christ as Savior. I'm to love God. I'm to obey Him. Isn't that work on my part?" No. It's a response to that which He has initiated and fully completed. Your very ability to respond in faith is based upon His objective work in the shed blood of Jesus Christ and the resurrection from the dead, and His divine enablement that releases you to respond in faith. The Gospel is God breaking into your life. It is not you reaching up to Him.

Your right relationship with God, which makes all things work together for good, has nothing to do with your good works. The one who has accepted Christ's invitation of salvation, however, is one who wants to please his Lord.

One night at dinner a young lady said to me, "I am really a very good person. Granted, I don't often go to church, but I'll guarantee that in God's eyes I'm just as good as a lot of those pious people who pretend to be so religious." That's not the issue — how good you are. The issue is whether or not you have responded to the call of God upon your life. The person who has accepted God's call is one whose life is marked by a sense of his own unworthiness in the light of God's holiness. The man or woman who has accepted the call of God has not done so because they believe in a deterministic kind of philosophy. It is because they have acknowledged the sovereignty of God.

Once the perspective is found and the conditions are met, then your life can be lived in the presence of the affirmation that all things do work together for good. This doesn't mean that you'll live a perfect existence. You will sin. But you also will live in the dimension of the confession of sin in which you yearn continually for the cleansing blood of Jesus Christ to wash away the sludge from your existence.

We know that all things do work together for good if you love God, if you are called according to His purpose. Even the puzzling and seemingly tragic things of life become His vehicle of spiritual power. That broken romance can protect you for the right marriage partner. That financial crisis can be the humbling experience that brings you to an awareness of your daily need of Jesus Christ. That death of a loved one can bring the tender touch of eternity into your life. That rebellious child can draw you closer to the feet of the Master who can give you patience and understanding. That Mongoloid child born to Dale Evans Rogers became an "angel unaware." Those blind eyes for Fannie Crosby opened dimensions of spiritual insight that enabled her to pen the words "Blessed assurance, Jesus is mine! Oh, what a foretaste of glory divine." The seemingly tragic jungle murder of five stalwart young missionaries to Ecuador has enabled scores of Auca Indians to be transformed so as to walk "Through Gates of Splendor."

Dr. Robert Holland of the Shadyside Presbyterian Church in Pittsburgh, Pennsylvania, stated this whole theme so succinctly when he said, "The Bible does not say the good will not suffer. It says the Lord will be with them when they do." That's the key to understanding the reality of God's promise that all things do work together for good. He takes the pain, the difficult, the impossible, and walks with you through them, transforming your whole perspective on life.

The essence of a surrendered life is the knowledge, the confidence, that all things do work together for good in God's eternal plan to those who love Him, to those who are called according to His purpose.

Your Impregnable Position 17

No, in all these things we are more than conquerors
through him who loved us. For I am persuaded that
neither death, nor life, nor angels, nor principalities,
not things present, nor things to come, nor powers,
nor height, nor depth, nor anything else in all creation,
will be able to separate us from the love of God in
Christ Jesus our Lord (Romans 8:37-39).

PAUL BEGAN his letter to the Romans by declaring, "For I am not ashamed of the gospel: it is the power of God for salvation to every one who has faith, to the Jew first and also to the Greek" (Romans 1:16). The theme of this book is justification by faith.

Paul then devotes a major part of chapters 1, 2, and 3 to showing God's righteousness and His wrath against all unrighteousness.

In Romans 3:21, Paul makes a major transition as he declares what God has done for us in Christ Jesus, enabling us to come to faith. Those of us who do repent of sin are persons clothed in Christ's righteousness. It's not our faithfulness to the law that saves us. It is God's gift. Abraham is used as a case example. As good a man as he was, he often sinned. It was only as he put his trust in the Lord that he became numbered as one of the great heroes of the faith.

In chapter 6 to the end of chapter 8, Paul describes the equipment God gives us to live the Christian life. It is the power of the Holy Spirit. It's not a life free from struggle. However, it can be a life of victory. We are not left to our own resources. We have a spiritual energy that enables us to live the way God created us to live.

When you and I come to the full realization of who we

are, who God is, and what God has done for us — and as we receive it as our own — we can claim our impregnable position. I love that word impregnable. It means invulnerable to capture. Unconquerable. Unassailable. It means "incapable of being taken by assault."

The largest pyramid in Egypt is Cheops. This giant, man-made mausoleum reaches 465 feet into the air. Huge granite blocks were transported many miles at an enormous cost of human life. Each of the several-ton stones fits into place. Cheops was an ancient monument when Moses looked upon it as a boy. It has stood impregnable through the millennia. Armies have marched past it. Its country has been captured and recaptured. It has been exposed to the elements. It still stands impregnable through these 5000 years.

This is precisely what you can claim as the result of what God has done for you in Jesus Christ. Yours is an impregnable position in which you can declare, "We know that in everything God works for good with those who love him, who are called according to his purpose" (Romans 8:28).

I

Why is it that you and I wrestle so much with God's sovereignty? One reason is that we still have a selfish nature. Romans 8:5-6 reminds us of our tendency at times to set our minds on the flesh instead of on the Spirit of God. When we do this we become hostile to God. We want things done our way. We have plans that are *our* plans for *our*selves, not *His* plans. We resent the fact that God doesn't seem to take our plans into account. We want what we want when we want it the way we want it. How could God dare not meet our selfish agendas?

Another reason some of us wrestle so much with God's sovereignty and have a difficult time claiming His promise is that we are afraid. We are victimized by the present order in which we live. In Chapter 15 we talked about how all creation is groaning. It is going through the process of travail that Paul describes in Romans 8:18-27. This groaning stage is what the residents in the Mount St. Helens environs have experienced. They don't know what to expect next. There have been groanings, eruptions, and showers of volcanic ash. The residents of the area look forward to a day when everything will once again be stabilized. That day may be close. It may be far away. In the meantime, there is disruption of business as usual.

We sense it economically as the OPEC nations continue to call for new price increases. Where will it all end? We feel this disruption as we watch the interest rates fluctuate up and down, as we observe our economy caught in what some call "stagflation." We feel the groanings in the international realm as the somewhat democratic West vies with the communist world. Now the third world of developing nations joins in with its plea to be heard. The Arab/Jewish tensions increase. Our family lives are unsettled. It's a threatening scene. We don't fully claim the promise because we are afraid as we wait for God's coming consummation of all human history.

Another reason that we have a difficult time acknowledging God's sovereignty and claiming his various promises to us is that we have a tendency to focus on the immediate, while God focuses on the ultimate.

You and I tend to function in a similar way to the flea on a carpet made up of multicolored squares. It is actually quite attractive when viewed from an adult vantage point. However, the little flea has a distorted perspective. At first he settles on the one-foot square red piece and is convinced that the entire carpet is red. That is the only color he can see. After a while he hops around over to the green square. When questioned as to the color of the carpet, he declares forcefully that the carpet is green. Then he hops to a yellow square. The whole carpet now looks yellow. His problem is that he tends to focus on the immediate. He can't see the broader picture of the multicolored carpet.

Dump a thousand-piece jigsaw puzzle on the table without ever having seen the master picture and you'll find yourself quite confused, won't you? You'll look first for the corner pieces. Then you'll fill in the sides. Gradually a picture will begin to take shape. When the whole puzzle is put together you'll have a sense of satisfaction. For us the puzzle has not yet been completed. We find it difficult to say that in everything God works for good.

While serving a church in Pittsburgh I had the opportunity to host a television talk show. On one show I was privileged to have Corrie ten Boom as a guest. Corrie is a magnificent Christian woman. She has received wide recognition for her efforts on behalf of the Jews during the Holocaust. She and her sister paid for their Christian humanitarianism by being thrown into a Nazi concentration camp. There, Corrie watched her sister die. It was only by a strange twist of God's providence that she was finally released. When I quizzed her as to how she could possibly have survived emotionally, physically, and spiritually through that horrendous experience, she opened her purse and pulled out some needlepoint. She held the back toward me and the camera and said, "What does this look like?" It looked like one big mass of miscellaneous threads. They made no sense. Then she turned it around and showed us a beautiful crown that she had been stitching. When we are caught up in the immediate, life looks like a jumble of threads, whereas there is an ultimate design of the Creator, a pattern that is glorious.

II

I can't answer all the problems of free will versus the sovereignty of God. I can make the statement that yours and mine is an impregnable position as we commit our lives to Jesus Christ. But I can't fully explain the topic of predestination to which Paul refers.

But I can tell of one great truth that will shed some helpful light on the subject. Paul has stated, "For those whom he foreknew he also predestinated to be conformed to the image of his son, in order that he might be the first-born among many brethren. And those whom he predestined he also called; and those whom he called he also justified; and those whom he justified he also glorified" (Romans 8:29-30).

If you have repented of sin, you are a "person of destiny." Psychologists warn us about megalomaniac tendencies. They alert us to the dangers of viewing oneself as a "person of destiny." This is a valid danger. In fact, the Bible warns us not to think more of ourselves then we ought to think. We can end up self-centered and proud, elevating ourselves above others. Jesus said, "He who would be first shall be the last."

At the same time, the Scriptures warn us about having low self-esteem. Even as we're not to have a superiority complex, we are not to think of ourselves as totally worthless. We are someone special to God. He is interested in us. We are not just an accident. We are His special creation, taking our places alongside all of His other special, special people.

You may enter into lengthy debate over some of the other implications of predestination. But one fact is not debatable. If you take the Scripture seriously, you are destined for heaven. This destiny is known in advance. It is based on a gift freely given and freely received. And not only are you destined for heaven in the life beyond this life. You right now have eternal life. God loves you. God is interested in you. Jesus said that not a sparrow falls from the sky but what your Father in heaven is aware of it. The very hairs on your head are numbered. You are a person known to God, a person whose present and future are secure. You are predestined.

A question. What is the most dangerous heresy in the world today? What error is destroying the most lives?

Your immediate reaction may be communism. I agree that communism is terrible, although it has some things to commend itself in its idealistic form. When fleshed out as we've seen it in Russia and China, it deprives people of their basic human rights. Even as some idealistic American scholars sit in their ivory towers, examining the deficiencies of capitalism while proselytizing the merits of Marxist ideology, we see no great rush of immigrants toward Cuba, Russia, or China, do we? But communism is not the greatest heresy in the world.

In the spiritual area, you may say that humanism is the greatest heresy. A critical humanism denies the deity of Christ, stripping Christianity of its supernatural content. Jesus becomes just another man, highly motivated and ethical in His teachings. We see people grabbing at this kind of religion. As seriously deficient as is humanism, there's a greater heresy.

The greatest of heresies is that salvation is based on what you do for God instead of what God has done for you. It has a way of making its inroad right into the very church of Christ. Christianity is not just obeying the Golden Rule and the Ten Commandments. This obedience is the spin-off of a love relationship between you and God. If I told you about a husband and wife in which the husband only gives the wife money for her household account after she gives him sex, you'd say that's not love, that's prostitution. You're absolutely right. And any one who thinks he can win his way into God's favor by buying Him off, purchasing salvation by good works, is trying to prostitute Almighty God.

Tithes and offerings, faithful church attendance, and community involvement, are simply spin-offs of the meaningful relationship you have with Jesus Christ. He gives you the free gift of forgiveness. This is what grace is all about. Jesus Christ did not come to make bad people good. Jesus Christ came to make spiritually-dead people alive. The prodigal son ripped off his father, took his inheritance, went to a far country, sowed his wild oats, and ended up feeding pigs. He came to his senses, repenting of what he had done. He returned home. What did his father say? "My son who was once dead is now alive." Jesus came to give you life. If you have received that life you are a person of destiny.

III

Paul concludes the first eight chapters of Romans with some summary verses. He starts out, "What then shall we say to this? If God is for us..." (Romans 8:31). At first glance, this looks like a question. Actually, it is a statement of your impregnable position. The phrase "If God is for us" deserves not a question mark but an exclamation point. It is saying in no uncertain terms that the message of the first eight chapters of Romans is simply "God is for us!" "God is for you!"

God has accepted you. He has always loved you. He is searching you out.

If then God is for us, what shall we say? Paul now addresses four rhetorical questions. Each of them is based on the fact that God is for you.

Question One. "If God is for us, who is against us?" (Romans 8:31).

Paul answers his own question with these words: "He who did not spare his own Son but gave him up for us all, will he not also give us all things with him?" (Romans 8:32). One of our neighbors put on a big celebration for their son's eighteenth birthday. The son was given a new car. It was the talk of the neighborhood. There was that car, sparkling clean, sitting in the middle of the front yard. Scores of guests were invited to the party. A band played. Every so often the guests would come out and admire the car. What would you think if the car had no hubcaps and the son asked the father, "Are you going to get hubcaps for the car?" "Are you serious? What do you want — some kind of a free ride? What are you, a spoiled kid? If you want hubcaps for your car go out and earn them!" It's pretty improbable, isn't it? Any father who is going to put all of the expense into buying a car for his son isn't about to quibble over four hubcaps.

Paul is saying the same thing about God's generosity toward us. He's saying do you think that God, the very God who gave His own Son for you, after making that sacrifice, is going to stop short of providing for you? After having made the biggest sacrifice of all, having paid the ransom to the kidnapper Satan, do you think He's going to leave you out on the street to fend for yourself? After releasing you from that international criminal, do you think He's going to throw you out on the street to the neighborhood thugs?

Question Two. "Who shall bring any charge against God's elect?" (Romans 8:33).

Your trial is over. God will not open a hearing in any case that will bring you into eternal jeopardy. He's aware that you're making mistakes. He's aware that you're not perfect. You're involved in a process of sanctification. He may discipline you. He may even at some point punish you. But he's never going to say, "Go to your room and don't come out until you're good." That's just not God's approach. He's a loving father who is prepared to nurture and encourage you. God is the one who justifies you. You're not justifying yourself. You're part of the family.

Question Three. "Who is to condemn?" (Romans 8:34).

Paul's response to this rhetorical question is fascinating. The Scriptures tell us that Jesus is the judge, the only judge. You and I have no right to judge another. We can only declare His word. We can call men and women to repentance in faith, but the only judge is Jesus. In response to this question, "Who is to condemn?" Paul responds, "It is Christ Jesus who died, yes, who was raised from the dead, who is at the right hand of God, who indeed intercedes for us" (Romans 8:34). Yes, Jesus is the judge. But interestingly enough, He is no longer your judge. He is now on your side. He is the defense attorney. This one has died and risen from the dead for you. He sits at the right hand of God the Father. He now makes intercession for you. He is your advocate. You are justified. That's what Paul means in Romans 8:1 when he says, "There is therefore now no condemnation for those who are in Christ Jesus." No one has the right to condemn you.

Question Four. "Who shall separate us from the love of Christ?" (Romans 8:35).

Paul then lists a number of temporal adversities. These are the things that make you and me feel separated from God's love. "Shall tribulation, or distress, or persecution, or famine, or nakedness, or peril or sword?" (Romans 8:35b). He's not promising us an easy life. You and I are going to have our difficulties. But the question is, will these difficulties ever separate us from the love of God? "No, in all these things we are more than conquerors through him who loved us" (Romans 8:37). He makes of you a conqueror. To be more than conqueror over tribulation is to be patient through it. To be more than conqueror over distress is to be master over the most difficult circumstances. To be conqueror over persecution is to be Christ-like toward the persecutor. To be conqueror over famine, or nakedness, or peril, or sword is to realize that your body may be killed, but you — the real you — survives.

Then Paul lists the spiritual powers. They were very real to the Christians of the first century, and perhaps they should be more real to us today. He says, "For I am sure that neither death nor life, nor angels, nor principalities, nor things present, nor things to come, nor powers, nor height, nor depth, nor anything else in all creation, will be able to separate us from the love of God in Christ Jesus our Lord" (Romans 8:38-39).

No power in the universe can permanently hurt a person who is in harmony with God through Jesus Christ. No matter how difficult your experience of life may be, nothing can separate you from his love as you yield yourself to Him. No extremes — life or death. No other order of beings — angels, principalities, or powers. No historic forces — things present or things to come. No astrological mysteries. Tear up your horoscope. Pay no attention to it. That's what it means when he says "nor height, nor depth." It means no matter how high your chart says your star is or how low it is, nothing predetermined by any other force, by any other creature, can separate you from the love of God in Christ Jesus, your Lord. Your position is impregnable.

CHRISTIAN HERALD ASSOCIATION AND ITS MINISTRIES

CHRISTIAN HERALD ASSOCIATION, founded in 1878, publishes The Christian Herald Magazine, one of the leading interdenominational religious monthlies in America. Through its wide circulation, it brings inspiring articles and the latest news of religious developments to many families. From the magazine's pages came the initiative for CHRISTIAN HERALD CHILDREN'S HOME and THE BOWERY MISSION, two individually supported not-for-profit corporations.

CHRISTIAN HERALD CHILDREN'S HOME, established in 1894, is the name for a unique and dynamic ministry to disadvantaged children, offering hope and opportunities which would not otherwise be available for reasons of poverty and neglect. The goal is to develop each child's potential and to demonstrate Christian compassion and understanding to children in need.

Mont Lawn is a permanent camp located in Bushkill, Pennsylvania. It is the focal point of a ministry which provides a healthful "vacation with a purpose" to children who without it would be confined to the streets of the city. Up to 1000 children between the ages of 7 and 11 come to Mont Lawn each year.

Christian Herald Children's Home maintains year-round contact with children by means of an *In-City Youth Ministry.* Central to its philosophy is the belief that only through sustained relationships and demonstrated concern can individual lives be truly enriched. Special emphasis is on individual guidance, spiritual and family counseling and tutoring. This follow-up ministry to inner-city children culminates for many in financial assistance toward higher education and career counseling.

THE BOWERY MISSION, located at 227 Bowery, New York City, has since 1879 been reaching out to the lost men on the Bowery, offering them what could be their last chance to rebuild their lives. Every man is fed, clothed and ministered to. Countless numbers have entered the 90-day residential rehabilitation program at the Bowery Mission. A concentrated ministry of counseling, medical care, nutrition therapy, Bible study and Gospel services awakens a man to spiritual renewal within himself.

These ministries are supported solely by the voluntary contributions of individuals and by legacies and bequests. Contributions are tax deductible. Checks should be made out either to CHRISTIAN HERALD CHILDREN'S HOME or to THE BOWERY MISSION.

Administrative Office: 40 Overlook Drive, Chappaqua, New York 10514
Telephone: (914) 769-9000